1982

From A to Z
200 Contemporary American Poets

From A to Z
200 Contemporary American Poets

200 Poets from *New Letters* Magazine

Edited by David Ray

A New Letters Book

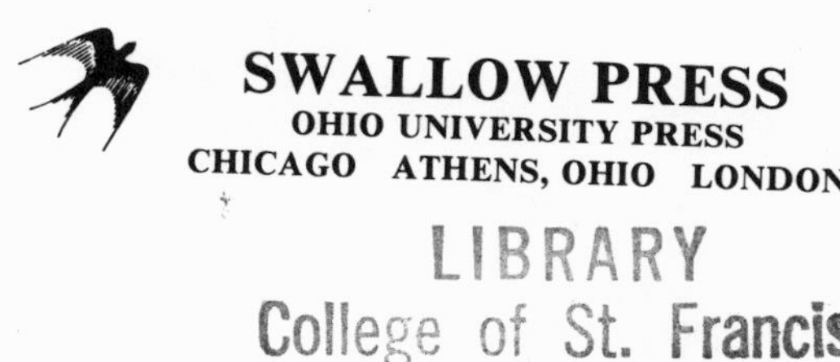

SWALLOW PRESS
OHIO UNIVERSITY PRESS
CHICAGO ATHENS, OHIO LONDON

Calligraphy by Lloyd J. Reynolds

Design by Judy Ray

Photo by Lewis Carroll on page 132 courtesy of the Humanities Research Center, University of Texas—Austin.

Library of Congress Cataloging in Publication Data
Main entry under title:

From A to Z.

"A New letters book."
Consists of poems which first appeared in New letters.
I. American poetry—20th century. I. Ray, David, 1932-
II. New letters.
PS615.F69 811'.52'08 80-27328
ISBN 0-8040-0369-6 (Swallow)
ISBN 0-8040-0370-X (Swallow : pbk.)

Swallow Press Books
are published by
Ohio University Press
Athens, Ohio

CONTENTS

1 William Carlos Williams
3 A. R. Ammons
4 Ray Amorosi
5 Alison Baker
6 John Balaban
6 Mary Barnard
7 Jim Barnes
10 Aliki Barnstone
11 Willis Barnstone
12 Tom Bass
14 Charles G. Bell
14 Marvin Bell
15 Albert Bellg
16 Bruce Berlind
17 Daniel Berrigan
17 Duff Bigger
18 Robert Bly
18 George Bogin
19 Philip Booth
20 Shirley Bossert
21 Alan Britt
22 Joseph Bruchac
23 John Cain
24 Hayden Carruth
27 G. S. Sharat Chandra
28 Henry Chapin
30 Josephine Clare
31 James Cole
32 Elliott Coleman
34 Horace Coleman
35 Victor Contoski
35 Izora Corpman
37 Bruce Cutler
37 Philip Dacey
39 Robert Dana
41 Dennis Dibben
41 Martha Dickey
42 William Dickey
43 Stephen Dunn
44 Stephen Dunning
45 Quinton Duval
47 Richard Eberhart
48 Frederick Eckman
49 W. D. Ehrhart
50 Larry Eigner

George P. Elliott 51
Harley Elliott 53
Greg Field 54
Edward Field 54
Dennis Finnell 55
Isabella Gardner 56
Dan Gerber 58
David Ghitelman 58
Chris Gilbert 58
Robert Gibb 59
Gary Gildner 60
Robert Gillespie 63
Daniela Gioseffi 64
Malcolm Glass 65
Patricia Goedicke 66
Paul Goodman 71
Arthur Gregor 72
Horace Gregory 73
Alvin Greenberg 74
Andrew Grossbardt 75
Daniel Halpern 76
Mark Halperin 77
Alfred Starr Hamilton 77
Tom Hanna 78
Kenneth O. Hanson 78
Donald Harington 79
Michael S. Harper 80
Stephen Harrigan 82
William Hathaway 83
Samuel Hazo 83
Tom Hennen 84
Ruth Herschberger 86
Geof Hewitt 87
Jeanne Hill 88
Pati Hill 88
Michael Hogan 90
Jonathan Holden 91
Anselm Hollo 92
Jim Howard 93
Richard Hugo 95
Lewis Hyde 96
Wang Hui-Ming 97
David Ignatow 118
Colette Inez 120
Charles Itzin 121

122 Josephine Jacobsen
123 Dan Jaffe
124 Thomas Johnson
125 Richard Jones
126 William Joyce
126 Arno Karlen
129 Dave Kelly
131 David Kherdian
133 Galway Kinnell
134 Etheridge Knight
135 Norbert Krapf
136 John Knoepfle
137 Maxine Kumin
138 Randy Lane
139 Denise Levertov
141 Philip Levine
144 Larry Levis
145 Crystal MacLean
145 Thomas McGrath
147 Joe-Anne McLaughlin
148 Sally McNall
148 Gerard Malanga
149 J. J. Maloney
150 Freya Manfred
156 Marya Mannes
157 E. L. Mayo
162 Mbembe Milton Smith
164 Robert Mezey
165 Vassar Miller
167 Ralph J. Mills, Jr.
168 Virginia Scott Miner
169 Frederick Morgan
169 Edward Morin
170 Hilda Morley
171 John W. Moser
172 Howard Moss
173 G. E. Murray
174 Tom O'Grady
175 Dave Oliphant
177 Elder Olson
178 Anthony Ostroff
180 Robert Pack
182 Philip Parisi
182 Linda Pastan
183 Karl Patten
184 Robert Peterson
185 Roger Pfingston
187 Frank Lamont Phillips
188 Felix Pollak
189 David Posner
189 Alan Proctor
190 Paul Ramsey
190 Rush Rankin
191 Julian Lee Rayford
191 Carl Rakosi

David Ray 193
Judy Ray 194
Lloyd J. Reynolds 195
John C. Rezmerski 199
Raymond Roseliep 200
Harry Roskolenko 201
Larry Rubin 203
Vern Rutsala 203
Ralph Salisbury 204
Andrew Salkey 205
Ted Schaefer 206
James Schevill 207
Dennis Schmitz 208
Grace Schulman 209
Harvey Shapiro 210
Morty Sklar 211
Robert Slater 212
A. G. Sobin 213
William Stafford 214
Stephen Stepanchev 218
Bert Stern 219
Robert Stewart 220
Ann Struthers 221
Lucien Stryk 222
David Swanger 226
John Tagliabue 226
Stephen Tapscott 228
James Tate 229
John Taylor 229
Virginia R. Terris 231
Phyllis Thompson 232
Jim Trifilio 233
Melvin B. Tolson 234
Joseph Torain 237
Leslie Ullman 237
H. L. Van Brunt 238
Robert Vander Molen 240
Byron Vazakas 241
Mark Vinz 241
Arturo Vivante 243
Linda Wagner 244
David Wagoner 245
Diane Wakoski 246
David Walker 248
John Wheatcroft 249
Sylvia Wheeler 250
Heather Wilde 251
Frederic Will 252
Jonathan Williams 253
Robert Willson 254
Harold Witt 254
Valerie Worth 255
Charles David Wright 256
Paul Zimmer 257
Richard Wright 258

"since feeling is first . . ."
e. e. cummings

Introduction

Definitions of poetry are as varied as hybrids of roses. "Poetry is not the thing said but a way of saying it," wrote A. E. Housman, with his famous rubric: " . . . if a line of poetry strays into my memory, my skin bristles so that the razor ceases to act. This particular symptom is accompanied by a shiver down the spine; there is another which consists in a constriction of the throat and a precipitation of water in the eyes . . . " One of my favorite poets, the late E. L. Mayo, casually referred to the act of creation: "To make a poem / You just grab hold of a word / Sticking out of your mind / And keep pulling." Interviewers want to know of poets two basics: 'What age did you begin writing?' is always the first question, and 'Can you *make* it happen or does it just *happen*?' is the gist of the second. Mayo describes his typical poem as "nothing but a snarl / Soft as velvet, a round / Greyish green hullabaloo / With a hole in the middle."

Nothing in the invidious dialectic of contemporary criticism has helped me understand poetry so well as such modestly offered comments from real poets. "For me poetry is like skiing, it can or cannot be competitive but it is always exhilarating. I find writing poems cheaper and in many ways more hazardous," writes William Hathaway, while Allen Ginsberg dismisses the whole process as "fried shoes." Randall Jarrell described the poet as a man who stands out in lightning storms. If he gets hit by lightning more than half a dozen times he's a great poet.

Poets know that their basic needs for creation are simple: tolerance, love, and as much freedom to express themselves as is enjoyed by dancers, swimmers and painters. A little less suffering and a few more positive strokes would not hurt them at all.

What many of them do not quite understand is the well-intentioned efforts of certain critics who reward sloppiness and drunken self-indulgence, who seem to take the worst and make it sound like the best. Such critics make sloppiness sound like genius. And when criticism encourages the worst, many living poets respond like Kafka's hunger artist, experiencing a terrific need to tell us where it hurts. They cannot understand the elevation of work that doesn't move them. They do not know why the star system with its superstars and academy awards, and other games of the art market, seem to have been transferred wholesale to the world of poetry. In such a time poets grieve because they have lost touch with those happy impulses that made them poets. They find the smog of much over-rated writing and the critical nonsense that deifies it as bewildering and noxious as any other form of double-think. In expressing the need to escape or protest, they long for the bitter gestures poets have traditionally made. One feels like Sherwood Anderson when he walked away from his job and headed out of town, walking along the railroad track. Another feels like Robinson Jeffers who went to Carmel by the sea, built his house stone by stone with his own hands and studied the hawk, in whose flight he searched for help in his own quest for truth. But few attain such purity of gesture. Most of us do indeed live lives of quiet desperation until the rough edges of individuality and variety are honed smooth. The schools and leagues of poetry become defined as foolishly and in as inbred a fashion as they did in the Eighteenth Century. The real poet flunks the groupie test. He is as bewildered trying to get along with the local workshop or the favor-swapping club members hanging around a particular magazine or university as if he had been invited to put on a logo T-shirt and compete in a donkey ballgame. And if the poet himself is a victim of confusion and *anomie*, God helped the poor reader who tries to sort it all out!

And yet poetry is thriving. Poets survive the negation and discouragement which they face and they go on working. Like Faulkner's Dilsey they can sometimes be said not only to survive but to prevail. Indeed, the comparison with Faulkner's black maid in *The Sound and the Fury* may be an apt one, for poets do seem to suffer from discrimination of many kinds. Our society offers a certain cool and ironic praise for the product poets deliver with sacrifices tantamount to life blood, and yet seems to offer poets little real love or interest in their survival; in fact, a cultish praise even glorifies suicide. The poet tries to achieve an almost transcendent understanding, an I-Thou relationship with the reader, but all too often, the real experience is of more rejection, misunderstanding. Here is where critics could help. But instead even the voicing of conscience sometimes earns the poets more contempt and neglect, as if their own seriousness were defined by how completely they can ignore the real world. There seems to be a high premium on indifference, while narcissistic self-concern—what kids used to call "cool"—is a treasured stance. For years one would not have known from the pages of at least one of our leading poetry journals that such realities as the Vietnam war, nuclear bombs, starvation, fallout and radiation hazards, etc. even exist. Poets who respond with concern still pay a high price for their convictions, while those who are proud of no concern at all seem to be darlings of the critics.

Anselm Hollo writes: "There is a great deal of exciting new writing in the U.S. today—especially in poetry & short fiction. As far as I can see, none of it is 'regional' in any significant sense . . . It strikes me that all the contemporary & younger poets whose work keeps me on my aging toes are 'eccentric' . . . precisely because they do not believe in any 'center of cultural imperialism'—never have, never will. So I write what keeps me entertained in the fullest sense of that verb. A relaxed commitment to the 'mind-graph moving' (Whalen); to language, & all conceivable languages, as the prime material; to 'accurate observation plus good humor' (Zukovsky); to surprise; to great big or tiny delicate piñatas of words—whap, wow! . . . There's no stopping us poets, you see. We'll stop only after—a little while after—the whole show is over." For those who feel, struggle, and necessarily express the vulnerability poetry has always exacted, all survival techniques must be kept active. Humor is basic. In "Businessman's Lunch" Tom Hanna writes: "What Happens when poets / get together to discuss business? We decided that the broken angels / were more viable than tethered goats."

A single book or magazine can do little to remedy the present state of American poetry. But just as writers can do no better than keep writing, no matter what, so editors can respond only by publishing the best work they can find. My own editorial criterion has always been a simple and intuitive one, though everything I have read, thought, or felt becomes involved: if I feel that a work is a sincerely felt experience and expressed with artful and persuasive techniques that move me, I will publish it. I have my own pet prejudices, of course, though I call them convictions; they guide me as an editor.

I do not pretend that the work here or in ongoing issues of *New Letters* is all great or immortal, nor do I offer a school of poetry. This book is a miscellany, a reader; it in no way replaces the full range of material available in past and ongoing issues of *New Letters*, the magazine that first published all this material. It is my hope that the reader will enjoy the variety and indeed feel that a kind of union of opposites has been achieved. But no attempt is made to offer a doctrinal umbrella or to be fully representative of all that is going on in American poetry.

Though no school of poetry is here represented other than one accidentally constituted, the poems here represent a wide range of interests, regional origin and aesthetic sensibility. Poets like Melvin B. Tolson, Etheridge Knight, Mbembe, and Horace Coleman represent the minority experience. Poets of the Northwest, like Mary Barnard, William Stafford, Anthony Ostroff, Vern Rutsala and Ralph Salisbury are present, along with those from the New England area like Maxine Kumin, Denise Levertov, Wang Hui-Ming, Geof Hewitt and Hayden Carruth. Philip Levine and Quinton Duval sent us their poetry from California; Dave Oliphant and Vassar Miller live in Texas, as do Steve Harrigan and Leslie Ullman. Josephine Jacobsen, Linda Pastan and others live along the East coast. Marya Mannes, David Ignatow, Harvey Shapiro, Harry Roskolenko, Ruth Herschberger, Daniela Gioseffi, Colette Inez, Howard Moss and many others are New Yorkers, while Josephine Clare, Dave Kelly, Valerie Worth, Joseph Bruchac and George P. Elliott live Upstate there. Patricia Goedicke has lived in Mexico for years and Pati Hill maintains a home in Paris. Alfred Starr Hamilton is famous for his boarding house poverty in New Jersey. Sharat Chandra, originally from India, now lives in Florida. Andrew Salkey, now living in Amherst, is originally from Jamaica. And there are those poets of the Midwest, whom Lucien Stryk has admirably described in his valuable *Heartland II* anthology (Northern Illinois University Press): "It's a wonder they hang on, out there in the boondocks, wringing poems out of whatever they can, but they do, and are the better for it—even if at times they doubt themselves." These poets include Crystal MacLean, Linda Wagner, Dan Jaffe, Freya Manfred, Robert Bly, Tom McGrath, Jim Barnes, Larry Levis, Harley Elliott and Gary Gildner.

I am grateful to many who have helped *New Letters* emerge as a regular outlet for new work, especially to Alexander Cappon, whose many years of effort with *The University Review* and *The University of Kansas City Review*, provided a tradition from which our editorial variation could take off. My wife, Judy Ray, who named the magazine in 1971, has been such a force that I can truthfully say the magazine would not have achieved the stability it has without her full involvement in every kind of decision. Robert Stewart has offered loyalty and patience as well as full intellectual involvement with the magazine's development. To these two I owe debts beyond paying. To the late calligrapher-poet Lloyd J. Reynolds, whose spirit blessed us with its powerful presence from the first days when we were designing and planning the magazine (and whose work we are sharing with you in this book), I owe continued reverence and respect. To all those within the University of Missouri-Kansas City who have been helpful and forebearing, we at *New Letters* are appreciative. They have not nagged us and they have let us get on with doing the best we can, and they have not been vindictive about our mistakes. To those writers who have let us get to know them as friends as well as colleagues we are thankful. Of these I would like to mention a very particular debt to Gary Gildner, whose own anthology, *Out Of This World* (still in print with Northern Iowa University Press), is a classic. Gary Gildner has not only been a friend, fellow-writer, and frequent contributor to *New Letters*, but also was co-editor of our special poetry issue of Summer, 1976, which was the forerunner of this collection. He was also a major advisor for the selection here, though I must excuse him from blame for any omissions, and, I hope, from some of the agonizing that goes with making final selections. Finally, a special note of thanks is due to Ernest and June Bartlett of Bartlett Typesetting for their patience and skill in working with the magazine and this book.

But it is you, dear reader, whom I thank most of all. For if Walt Whitman ever said a truth, it was that to have great poets we must have great audiences. If you care for these poems and if a few of their lines resonate at some unlikely time in your mind these poets will have accomplished their life's work. As Walt Whitman put it, the poet is saying to you, "Be careful of this—it is my *carte de visite* to posterity."

—DAVID RAY
Kansas City, Missouri, 1980

A fame
that is to last
a thousand years
will rise after
an unappreciated life
is past

TU FU

William Carlos Williams

A Sort of a Song

Let the snake wait under
his weed
and the writing
be of words, slow and quick, sharp
to strike, quiet to wait,
sleepless.

—through metaphor to reconcile
the people and the stones.
Compose. (No ideas
but in things) Invent!
Saxifrage is my flower that splits
the rocks.

The Aftermath

The Winnah! pure as snow
courageous as the wind
strong as a tree
deceptive as the moon

All that is the country
fitted into you
for you were born there.
Now it is rewarding you

for the unswerving mind
curious as a fox
which fox-like escaped
breathless to its hole.

They say you have grown
thinner and that
there is a girl now to
add to the blue-eyed boy.

Good! the air of the
uplands is stimulating.

A. R. Ammons

Model

I refuse the breakage:
I hold on
to the insoluble knots
I've circled for years
turning in contradictory
wildness as
safe with center as
jugs and stars: what
I can't become keeps me
to its image: what
can't be reconciled is
home and steady at work.

Self-Projection

The driest place in the yard's
under the faucet:
where there is hose
length will be utilized
transporting the source away
from its own critical drought:
hesitate and undo: unscrew
and turn the undisciplined faucet
on: what more than the self
sometimes needs the self.

Ray Amorosi

Note in a Sanitorium

After he sledged wife the man
sliced his hand off in factory meat cutter.
There's a thin scar around his other wrist
like the mark a rubber band would leave—

That hand sewn back on, a shriveled
blue halo of a hand.

Under my right eye a lump and a knock
on the chest of an open body.
Mother died and father dead in sanitorium.

I promise I'll be a great man, a shadow
on the grass outside your cell window,
what else could you want a man
with no compulsion, no compulsion.
My father in sanitorium whose family a nightmare.

I have dream of world as cockwand.
I have dream of being in there myself and pointing
the mistake out with my stump.
Blue halo. Me. No hand, no wife, no song.

Alison Baker

Custer (1)

You, Custer, you hated
women too, didn't you—
ripping into warm red
flesh, mounting them
like horses, driving
them screaming into
the wars of your deserts;
you spewed your pale seed like teeth.
We reap them still,
sharp-faced golden
men, blond bones driving
through their thin flesh,
slashing with their swords
at soft stomachs and but-
tocks, charring darker
bodies with your
caucasian flames

Custer (2)

In this picture
Custer is wearing
the kind of boots I want.
They come all the way to his knees
and they have low heels.
They look as if they keep the rain out.
Custer is standing
with his left leg forward
and his right hip swung back,
his arms folded
and his hat at
a not-too-rakish angle.
There is a star on his collar.
He looks thin under his uniform.
"All I need," he's thinking,
"is a little polish on these boots
and a shot of whiskey.
I think I'm the hot tuna."

John Balaban

After Our War

After our war, the dismembered bits
—all those pierced eyes, ear slivers, jaw splinters,
gouged lips, odd tibias, skin flaps, and toes—
came squinting, wobbling, jabbering back.
The genitals, of course, were the most bizarre,
inching along roads like glowworms and slugs.
The living wanted them back, but good as new.
The dead, of course, had no use for them.
And the ghosts, the tens of thousands of abandoned souls
who had appeared like swamp fog in the city streets,
on the evening altars, and on doorsills of cratered homes,
also had no use for the scraps and bits
because, in their opinion, they looked good without them.
Since all things naturally return to their source,
these snags and tatters arrived, with immigrant uncertainty,
in the United States. It was almost home.
So, now, one can sometimes see a friend or a famous man talking
with an extra pair of lips glued and yammering on his cheek,
and this is why handshakes are often unpleasant,
why it is better, sometimes, not to look another in the eye,
why, at your daughter's breast thickens a hard keloidal scar.
After the war, with such Cheshire cats grinning in our trees,
will the ancient tales still tell us new truths?
Will the myriad world surrender new metaphor?
After our war, how will love speak?

Holiday Inn, Oklahoma City
August, 1973

Mary Barnard

The Solitary

The lone drake, upended,
nibbles the pond bottom,
red legs paddling the air.

He sleeps on the rock wall
by the spillway, balanced
on one foot, head hidden.

In the shadowed shallows
under sycamore boughs
the encircling ripples

have one center: himself.
Intruders, including
mallards of his own race,

beautiful strangers, drive
him to frenzied attack,
quacking, snapping, churning

the pond. When they have gone
bright wavelets unbroken
to the rim spread round him.

Jim Barnes

Descent to Bohannon Lake

You leave the skyline
at the summit and drop
toward the blue water
a thousand feet below.

Who walked this way before
and down is written hard
on the face of every scree
and shattered. Descending

the trail circles the failing
ground. Light off such stones
stunts trees, vision. The bones
of shadow press ancient wings,

words, into the stones. You read
the why and how of going down
to Bohannon Lake
on this a hot summer's day.

Accident At Three Mile Island

" . . . how everything turns away/Quite leisurely . . . "
—W. H. Auden

The island steams under the opening sky.
All around the narrow length of land
the river flows as it always has, and late

birds heading north to Canada notice
nothing unusual about the air.
There may, or may not, have been a disaster

among the undergrowth: what birds may tell
is augured late at best, and fish homing
upstream are mainly interested in falls.

Who knows? At any rate the land was calm.
Nothing surprised farmers off their tractors
or knocked the rheumy cattle off their hoofs,

though something surely must disappear every
time the earth shakes or the sky moves an inch
or two to right or left. Still there will always

be a boy fishing from some river bank
who doesn't especially want anything to happen
except summer and a dog scratching at his side.

Judy Ray

Old Soldiers Home at Marshalltown, Iowa

No movement on the hill: the old soldiers
are dying, dying into mushrooms they dream.
On the grounds near the rising river, the slow
phallic plants grow white and low. The days
swell, and no one stoops to the task at hand.

The old soldiers are dying, dying into the spring:
statues turn green with the grass. The tavern
at 13th and Summit echoes this green death,
but there is no song of esprit de corps.
no body lying on the floor drunk on
a reverie of a Flander's field or Argonne.

Even the drugstore across from the gate
is as vacant as the eyes you sometimes see
at the dark windows on the hill. The years
have emptied Seberg's of more than wares.
Time was when Jean Seberg was a bedside name,
the darling of bored veterans and gossips in
this town, the star of Saturday matinees.

From the tavern stool, you listen to the whir
of the laundromat across the street washing
some lonely nurse's whites, spinning them free
of trenches, the soiled touch she's come to dread.
You know that you've got it wrong, dead wrong,
that life here is as vital as your organs.
But somewhere in your head the old soldiers
are dying, dying into the fullness of spring.

Aliki Barnstone

A Letter from the Hotel

for Marti, Riqui, and Jack

I'm starting to feel good
about waking up first,
ordering soft-boiled eggs and papaya
in Spanish, alone.
I was the only one who got sick.
Marti, Riqui, and Jack ordered
mineral water for me
and went to the market
while I stayed in a hotel room
with no nationality.
Day after day
we spiral on a tiny line
of mountain roads.
The buses here are asthmatic,
our driver believes he is psychic,
and I am getting mystic.
Everytime he speeds into the left lane
we shoot through the sky,
our wheels are on the gold edge
of the Guatamalan clouds,
and I'm thrilled,
certain that I am already dead.
The Indians wear cloths
jungled with colors, animals and flowers.
They throw bananas at me,
the *gringa* with her camera.
I want to stay,
balance a jug on my head,
and learn to weave.
At night in the hotel
my last Spanish words
are for another *agua mineral.*
I carry the tray to my bed,
relieved to be suddenly nowhere,
writing my own language,
brushing my blond hair.

Willis Barnstone

Rooftop

for my father
d. 1946

You jumped so long ago
now it seems you were
never really here. I know
you were and remember
vaguely. If you could
fly back up to the ledge
and show up today young
as you were, we would go
again out to the desert
or south of green Oaxaca
go on double dates.
We discovered what a window
was the afternoon we chased
bats from our jungle room;
and if I also live close to
the roof, we share a secret
of the good cells on fire
in our black lungs. One night
I failed you. I said no
I could not come. The phone
clicked. You sailed so long
ago out of this world
yet I can't find where
to put that love: the pear
sapling I let wither or
the avocado tree you tore
out of yourself and me.
Our love lay folded neatly
with your coat and felt hat
found on the rooftop
on the day you swan dived
and forgot to sail back up
in the high open sunny air.

The Worm

My fathers come to me in an old film:
a peddler and tailor in the new world;
in the old, the image blurs, unknown.
I must be a bit like them. Old photos
say, look, here you were with a white beard,
black hat, a dark faith in the One God.
But they stood dully in the light and were
despised. They wandered here. It seems
impossible—here where I work and now
a plane hangs like a shiny wasp
in the air. With no God or fear I am
a free son—with the worm eating my heart.

Tom Bass

Spring Sunday On Quaker Street

In a storm after the storm
two days after spring
I walk across the way
to hunt up a drill I need.

Inside his garage the neighbor tells me,
while his wife watches from an inside doorway,
the rear spring snapped, when she backed out
of her mother's drive in town
in the fourth-hand Ford,
coming home alone, late from the Legion
last night, with kids asleep
in the back seat. Eyes glazed, sulky, she leaves.
I forget what I came for.

Helpless on our backs,
what we see of the day
is what's to be done,
is done to fix what broke.

How many nuts to ease . . .
rust frozen, with a propane torch,
liquid wrench, cold chisel,
stone hammer, sledge
and 2 pieces of pipe for breaker bars.

Inside where it's not snowing in
we curse wind and snow, turning
on bare concrete
in an open farmhouse garage
fighting roadsalt, snow and sand
splashing down from a rusted frame
to get the broken spring off and put
one off a junk body from Carter's
back on, not having done it before.

Now working with a droplight
in a litter of borrowed tools.
Keen metallic ring of wrenches:
open end, box, socket, rachet,
pipe, extension, adjustable . . .

Took a log binder, trace chain,
2 pinch bars, to get her
lined back up and bolted on.

Walk home late after dark,
drill in my pocket I can't use
now, day not fit for words,
most of it working at rust,
the half-day it took two to do
what a friend said was a one man
job, two country mechanics working
fast to beat a spring sunday.

Charles G. Bell

Two Families

In rain-forest Chiapas, at the table of Chang,
American Gothic exhibits right from wrong.
The Iowa mission sends this virtuous couple
To demonstrate imperatives of the moral:
Who, hobbled, have grazed and scratched together
Thirty years without breaking a tether,
Exhort through lips like a pursed-up bag
(Categorical sabotage)
Our old forest Maya with his child-wife and child
And his old wives and children—and look, how they smile!

Marvin Bell

Coralville, in Iowa

Worldly skinflints! We have your home-
stead—remember the one you wanted:
This was under water. The sea life
shows up in your driveway gravel;
we think *corn* but crunch fossils.
Those little beings built a network
in a world without future, pride.
We know. Here we have their past.
Here in the plains at the seacoast
which was, we do think often
that the moon overturns us and stars point
just as they do for men far out at sea.
Lookers-up, sailors, men on duty sometimes
can be in several places at a time.
Risking a look back, here we can be
in several times in this place.
Then as now, a coral city
is rising from the hardest parts of us.

Albert Bellg

Raincoats for the Dead

They need them the most, she tells us, and we
believe her, imagining the dark spattered mounds of
eroding earth and the dust on the red tiled roof of
the mausoleum jolted into the air by a thousand
gentle blows. There is something religious about
them that prevents a soul from leaving its body.
What's so good about floating around? she says.
You'd be better off anchored to what you loved, with
all its personality. You'd remember the dry wind
blowing through your bedroom curtains, the rain
coming down in a distant orchard.

Watertower

A watertower is like a silver egg in its nest
of trees. You can imagine some of the hatchlings:
tea holders, toilet floats, depth charges.

But what really lives inside the steel walls?
Lynch mobs with flashlights, radio controlled
planes, and desperate salmon with, at last, no
place to go and facing death,

the beauty of it, the relief, the crying, the
deep thing floating up and breaking through.

For it rises slowly and bursts slowly and
showers down the silver water of evening.

And what is within approaches through the air.

And one you've always loved within yourself
awakens and says, Here it is, it's come for you —
and I'm going too, we'll go together.

And you drift out with it through the trees
and into the evening.

Bruce Berlind

Period Piece

I stand at the window
smoking. Across the room
you play "Claire de lune"
con affetto
on the grand piano.
You are resting
after yesterday's abortion.
Through a pane of old glass
(the only one not yet replaced)
cars drift noiselessly
slow-motion spectres in the silent snow.
You are wearing
a red house-gown
it is brocaded with gold
you are very beautiful.
When our eyes meet, the
ceiling soars like Amiens
the room
is elegant as Versailles, my
cigarette
sprouts a carved ivory holder
and I know
that we love each other
and that
we are the last
decadents characters
in a Lubitsch film
dumb
with adoration
like Wordsworth's nun.

Fragment

No use
being angry at the dead.

Bone
lash back?

Ash
stand reproved?

How dare they deserve?
Love, even.

Daniel Berrigan

Handicapped

and the least of these
a gull, a foolish gull
spreadeagled there

a serious longsuffering look
the wrinkled eyelids
sorrow beyond sorrow

the sea raging
the land
an autumnal wreath

and he
seeking with vigilant eye
to enter
in a cloud's rift
in an eye's wink
the kingdom of light

Duff Bigger

IT IS WHEN THE TRIBE IS GONE
and I sit within the circle of stones
and maintain the fire.
A dog gnaws on a bone
at my side.
The woods are full of deer.
That tapping that I hear is from my thumb
on my bow when I hear something
move. We are not safe here on this planet.
It is winter. The smoke above the fire
is getting dim.
On a night like this one Van Gogh dug in into his bla
and died

THE COMEDIAN SAID IT:
that talking to that girl
is like opening a door into the sea
and having the knob come off
in your hand

Robert Bly

Black Pony Eating Grass

Near me a black and shaggy pony is eating grass,
that crunching is night being ripped away from day,
a crystal's sound when it regains its twelve sides.

Our life is a house between two hills.
Flowers stand open on the altar,
the moonlight hugs the sides of popples.

In a few years we will die,
yet the grass continues to lift itself into the horse's teeth,
sharp harsh lines run through our bodies.
A star is also a stubborn man—
the Great Bear is seven old men walking.

George Bogin

The Visitor

It was storming and there was someone at the door.
It was Franklin D. Roosevelt in his wheel chair,
his crutch pointing at the bell. We wheeled him in
out of the night and placed him near the fire,
helping him off with his wet cape. He was older,
very solemn, very sad. He loosened his tie,
unbuttoned the vest of his rumpled fine suit,
removed his pince-nez and wiped them.
He talked of his great weariness
and of his long absence from the Republic.
We spoke with him as an accustomed friend
who had been in our house many times.
How good it was to see him again!

Troopship for France, War II

I paint you this:
black blue for the sea at night,
black for the hurrying ship,
red for the end
of the olive drab dreamers
over the white wake.

Philip Booth

Rout

The latitude frozen:
a road straight through
spruce wilderness,
91 miles due west
to a bunkhouse.

The treetrunk sign
at the road-end says
the same name as
the map: a turnaround
called *Philosophy.*

Some free spirit.

The plank bunks
squeak all night
with everybody's
best dream: the girl
who's waited ever
since highschool.
After the other crew
comes off the night
shift, the new guys
rig the strap on their
hardhats, polish off
one last muffin, and
gun it: that's what
the government sent
them to do: gun it,
flat out, straight
into the continent.

Shirley Bossert

At Arm's Length

It is a night
to hold out in front,
a night to take
a longer look
under the junebug's belly
that comes in May,
watch a plane
blink its way in between
those still stable stars
It is the kind of night
that coyote howling
over the next hill
might walk to my
glass door and
stare at me
and I would let him in.

Judy Ray

Alan Britt

After Spending All Day at the National Museum of Art

I draw your outline
on the air,
one high cheekbone
and two loose apples in your blouse.

An awkward word,
like a tiny white parachute
follows me everywhere I go.

Serenade

The frog will serenade
your wedding.

The night will dance
upon your four breasts.

The buildings all tremble
with dew.

An arm reaches
beside a window
and places your skull
behind the moon.

Joseph Bruchac

Coots

Small black birds
with yellow beaks
and legs set back
so far they almost
fall off their tails

they swim like a man
leaning into a strong wind

Today I have seen
hundreds of them
out in the Hudson,
secure from hunters' guns
for few shoot a bird
whose flesh tastes like mud

and so, close to the flow,
the coots survive.

The Narrows

On a granite boulder
just off the roadbed
of the New York Central
a black man in a red beret
fishes for striped bass,
his son playing on the rock behind him.

On either side of them
apple trees overflow
with pink blossoms.

And now the red fire in the sky
joins its rays
with the fire in the river,
twin magnets
drawing each other towards sunset.

Open

Milk weed pods
hold out their empty hands
by the road which leads
to the Airport
and the County Jail
but for thousands of
   miles, under January snow,
feathers of seed
have touched the Earth.

John Cain

At The Nursing Home

At the nursing home for the ill at ease
the orderlies no longer carry whips.
Who needs a whip when a stare will do.

The grounds are graveyards in which
the patients bury the future in the past.
It is quiet without a future or a past.

You know where you are going so you
never arrive. And the joy of packing
the present is enough. Almost, enough

24

Hayden Carruth

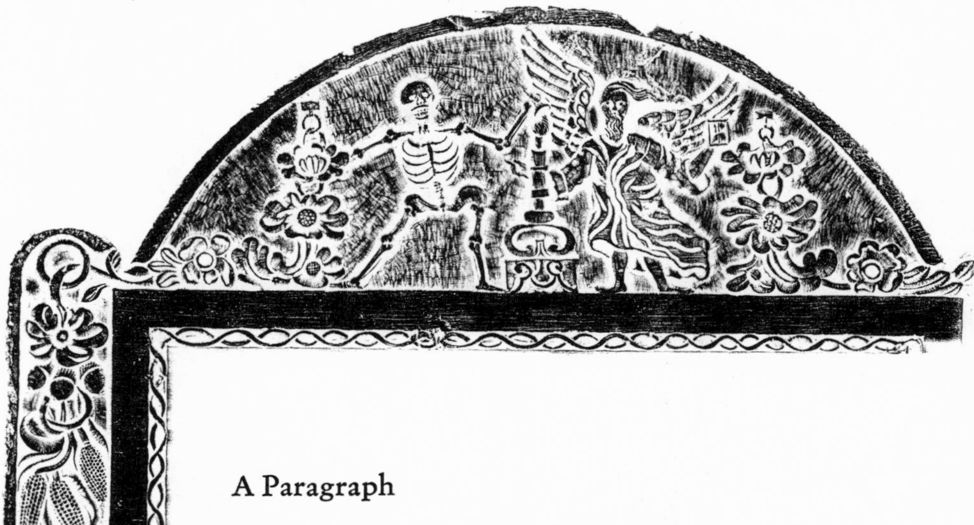

A Paragraph

I see you, brothers and sisters, Randall, John,
I see you all, Sylvia, Anne, your slow
ragged troupe wandering,
holding your flambeaux
so listlessly, calling, calling, your voices wan
and quavering. I hear you. Oh, it could be done
so quickly, you say, only a step,
a trigger's click, a drift of sleep,
that's what you sing—in that awful music of Moussorgsky,
in your valley of mist,
in your smoky flame-light, calling, calling to me.
Come, you sing, come to us, listen
to this singing here forever where you belong
in this valley, we are your brothers and sisters
only a minute away, a second, a song . . .

Privation

The longing to
make love is a
relentlessness
in the house with
bars over its
windows, so he
gazes, gazes
at the plumtree's
out-in-the-world
allure, bridal
at times or at
times fecund or
fiery, then chaste
and naked when
the snow comes, she
out there and he
melting against
bars, tortured. He
rises, swells, the
fury is on
him, but no, no,
he melts and he
goes down, bent on
his knees in a
kind of prayer, or
groveling or
weeping in the
spring, summer, fall,
and winter of
humiliation.

My Dog Jock

When I was a boy, perhaps
eight or nine, I read
how the Jesuits converted the
Indians, or left them "unconverted,"

and thereby discovered, suddenly
when I woke at the end of a night
and looked to the Connecticut hills
emerging in first light,

that though I was here I had
no right to be here,
but was born a stranger; and later
in church my unnamable fear

that came because I knew I did not
and could not believe in God,
told me the same thing on a larger
scale, the world belonged to God,

who was a great sachem whom I loved
more than King Arthur or Joan
or Ulysses but not as much
as my dog Jock, who was known

to me, known as I knew that what
I had been given was
something I had not asked for and might
never have asked for. Alas!

So I must say it, for only
the olden word will do.
And my dog Jock died
a long time ago,

and since then for forty-odd years
the earth has looked at me
with doglike hurt eyes,
accusingly,

and I have been alone, always
essentially alone,
like the Indians now, and God,
and everyone.

G. S. Sharat Chandra

In Praise of Blur

The old restlessness is gone
I'm the echo of my own wetness

O blur, glowing familiar
each minute,
do I choose to chase
or chase to choose your embrace?

You're the Shangrila
where philosophers grow exact
& jumbo jets fall in love

Is it your fault
the Germans lost the war
that poets on the low road
curse the interference?

I hear you hum,
on a clear day you can't see me
& the mirror bends backwards

I bet your body's silver
yet as I reach for a hug
I feel vague out of power

O astronomer tightening
on my wandering haze

You've brought me
the tranquillity of a snail
contemplating its snout . . .

Henry Chapin

A Quality of Air

There is a quality of air
in Greece. It can hang a mountain
lightly from the sky.
Goat bells, bird song,
a shepherd's distant horn,
filling the bowl of a valley,
will rest suspended,
as if they might be touched
and brought to hand.
Jewelled isles floating upon the sea,
strike the airs to music from their crowns.
Light is tangible, sounds take body.
Life is one. Icarus is.

Home here, the dusk takes over.
The crescent moon swinging from its star,
evokes the owl's drifting doom.
The flutes of the peepers ring, stop and start.
The sad monotony of whip-poor-wills
bemuse the night. It could be thought,
ours the older world.

Easy Does It

When very young
I learned to run.
At middle age
I built a cage.
And, like a squirrel,
spun in a whirl.

One day I saw
what I headed for,
was Marble Town.

I slowed me down.

Helpmate

When man, the pathfinder,
has lost the trail
and come full-circle
back upon himself,
the practical, enduring one
calls out: Make camp right here.
Chase me up some bacon,
bring it home and raise a shack,
while I cook and make the bed.
After, if you must,
you can talk of fate
and all that stuff.

Threes

Three fallen leaves chase
madly down the street.
Three eagles whistle and close
high in the blue.
Three raunchy dolphins
caper in one wave.
Three desperate souls
play at odd-man out.
Must everything resolve itself to two?

Josephine Clare

Fine Body

If memory were only in the head —

(do not sleep more than once
wth any one)

the body is a stupid redneck
you try to reason
bang! comes the fist
down on the table
the redneck sees red:
— get me that body   now!

the body is a crabby baby
that wants
wants with a vengeance
that body
the baby thinks that body
is the bottle
the baby goes on a fast
the baby says — i die on you
                        you'll be sorry

the body drags its feet
you put a thousand miles between
you & that body
the body keeps on begging
for that body

you give the body a body
you give it some *fine* body

the body does not want some fine body
it repulses it
but wants that body
that body from back there

the body throws tantrums
almost suffocates
gasps
for
air

we're unlucky

John Bowles

James Cole

The Wheel

All the time cold water fell
Into such leafy ruin—
A mill on fruitless soil,
The orphanage, the barracks

—Over its clear course
The little crossbones shook,
And men with weapons slept:
Bottles, rags, gelignite.

Elliott Coleman

Winter Over Nothing

The time of Nobody
And Nothing
Has come

Vestiges   Footprints

Of Beauty and Beauties

Fall in snow flakes
And soon are nothing
But unrecalled
Patterns

The Living are   Nothing
The Beloved are   finally   Nothing

O that Something so full of Something
Should turn out to be Nothing
Should turn inside out to be Nothing

In the Winter
In the Winter
Nothing

O that Somebody so full of Somebody
Should become   Nobody   Nothing

That one self should be no self
And the best thing be no thing

Winter   breathless   nothing

Snow us Under

Winter Over Nothing

Sirens

What should we do without the sirens
ambulance and fire
fearsome and delicious sense that
someone we do not know is suffering
maybe we know them
ah

Never so jabbed with contentment as
when we hear that sound
It reminds us of the non-air-raid signals we
long to perpetuate   hoping for
the real thing   and
the dishing of it out

Sirens
oh

The derivation of that word   and
what rocks

Judy Ray

Horace Coleman

Remembrance of Things Past

mortars are
the devil coughing
napalm?
Baudelaire never had
such flowers
such bright fleur de lis
such evil

claymores
shatter more than bones

when they attacked we
killed them dreams and all
we thought

we fired artillery they
shot hatred back

when we burned their bones
they loathed us still dying
still trying to get their crisp
black fingers on our white throats

A Black Soldier Remembers

My Saigon daughter I saw only once
standing in the dusty square
across from the Brink's BOQ/PX
in back of the National Assembly
next to the ugly statue of
the crouching marines facing
the face pond the VC blew up
during Tet.

The amputee beggars watch us.
The same color and the same eyes.

She does not offer me one of the
silly hats she sells Americans and
I have nothing she needs but the
sad smile she already has.

Victor Contoski

The Suicides of the Rich

In autumn
the rich all over the world
are burdened by their bodies.

They fold their Wall Street Journals
and look dreamily toward the horizon.

And pistols find their hands.
Injections caress their braceleted arms.
Waves wash their tailored suits.

Wherever you go in autumn
you hear the soft *plop plop*
of the bodies of the rich
falling falling falling.

Izora Corpman

The Photos From Summer Camp

Yes, eight, when
that was taken,
and was I certain

in my rolled jeans
and braids, bossy
and sunburned—

that's the summer
I led the parade.
There, we had piled

all the bedrolls—
the bus to take us
home was late. Here,

trying to look sweet,
we'd just beat the
boys at relays. And

when That One took
me in the woods to
trade looks at our

private things and
showed me his,
I said, "SO"

when I was 8.

Judy Ray

Bruce Cutler

Results Of A Scientific Survey

About mirrors in hotel rooms: one can say

French mirrors focus on the faces; below
    the armpits lies the mystery

The British aim them so that one sees only
    with great difficulty, at an angle

Russian mirrors do not reverse the image,
    of course

And Italians spread out, with loving attention
    to the parts

The German mirror is prescriptive, marked
    and calibrated where you ought to shine

But the Swiss, ah the Swiss mirrors,
    lucidity of plate glass, perfection
    of mercury,
    fleet images frozen forever.

Philip Dacey

The Ring Poem: A Husband Loses His Wedding Band as He Gestures From a Bridge

It was an accident, and accidents
Don't mean, of course, but still the wedding ring
Flew off my finger, down into the river.
It was so hard and small it fell all full
Of direction, not the way paper does,
Seemingly unsure it wants to fall,
But like a stone that knows its place is down
And down. Shocked, you and I could only watch.
Age thins my fingers, and the air was cold:
I'd meant to tape the ring that very morning
But there it was, on its own, a hurtling child.
The time it took falling was a mere flash;

In memory it seems a slow descent.
I see it now, all camera-slowed, lovely
Arc, fine fragment of what circle, and now
-stopped: see, a bead of shining, knot of light.
But let it fall. There, already it breaks
The water, like a baby, coming through.
In my end is my beginning and
So forth. We know all that. This was a ring,
Hard and cold, falling into water, no
More and no less. It wasn't any fish
That sucks now at bottom on river muck,
It wasn't any angel with clipped wings.
It was a ring, a wheel, a wife, a life,
It wasn't anything I understand,
It was a silver thing to catch for prize,
It told unbrokenness, and other lies,
Was silent, always, didn't say a word.
But you did. With your darkening eyes, said this:
"Was that I? I felt a fluttering here
In my being's center, as if I fell.
I've felt it before. It comes over me
Sometimes when I'm on the solidest ground—
A sense of gravity, and I am grave.
I've been falling for years. I'll keep falling,
No one can catch me. I think you fall with me
And that we shine in falling, like your ring."
The brown river snaked away under us.
It took the ring, and tried to take our faces,
But our faces held, dancing on the surface.
I took your hand, meaning to say by touch:
"What it was I lost just now, I don't know.
I expect never to know for certain.
But, in going away, whatever it was
Curved as if, given enough time and space,
It would return. Perhaps it will come back
Transformed beyond recognition, some new
Round thing bending the lines of our lives to it.
It shall be a kind of good encirclement."
Suddenly I felt my finger's nakedness.
I clasped my hands, then slipped them in my coat.
If you noticed, you didn't give any sign—
Except you picked up small stones from the bridge
and seeded the water with them, making rings.

Robert Dana

Mineral Point

These immigrant houses
full of clear dry light
face north and east

toward the vanished mouth of the mine

Dressed limestone
And a clear spring
that flows to the kitchen door

where we are told
by a girl whose face
shines like milk

how these Cornish miners
were windlassed by twos
in a wooden bucket

eighty feet down

to drift tunnels
and hack out lead and dry-bone
by candlelight

We have nothing
to love them for

Nothing to forgive

They grew humpbacked

And ate and drank
from tin pails filled with pasty
and water for hot tea

Perhaps they loved their wives

The night
that tumbled down the shafts to them
from Shake Rag St.

like a handful of coin

was the same darkness
that finds us
all naked under our clothes

the same darkness
that chattered beside them
like a stub of black candle

like the starling
in its wicker cage

Gary Gildner

Dennis Dibben

Some Modern Good Turns

(poem found in the 1936 Boy Scout Manual)

Helped the cook pick a chicken.
Cranked car for one-armed man.
Helped a paralyzed man fix his papers.
Took a small child across three streets.
Boy was sick, pulled him home on wheel.
Splinted and bandaged broken leg of dog.
Took chewing gum off the street-car seat.
Went to town to get husband for sick woman.
Removed slipknot from around cow's neck.
Attended to neighbor's baby while she went down town.
Made scrapbooks for the Home of the Friendless.
Climbed a tree at night to get a chicken for a lady.

Martha Dickey

Studies From Life

I'm looking through the paintings of Arthur Dove
his storms
the idea of storms
as seen from storm's eye.
Storms he knew, having left his family
for the woman he loved
to live with her in a small boat
on the ocean, the galley so low
they could not stand upright.
In winter when the storms got bad
they went inland to paint
the idea of storms.

William Dickey

Face-Paintings of the Caduveo Indians

The face-paintings of the Caduveo, says Levi-Strauss,
reflect a society they have forgotten;
like heraldry, he says, like playing cards.

It is like that. Even my mother, now,
turning the pages of the photograph album,
forgets the older faces. She insists she remembers,
but what she remembers is a style of face,
a way she can remember people looking.

I saw you at the Greek Orthodox church on Sunday.
You had lost weight. I was drinking sweetened coffee.
We were no longer a society.
I saw you as a stranger might, with interest.
You had drawn back behind the surface of your face.

In the last days, having nothing in common, we played cards,
and the cards became their own society,
playing themselves, not responsible to the players.
Your face became new, as if it had not been used.

I do not know what became of the Caduveo.
The face-paintings are in a museum, with the relics
of other societies that forgot themselves
that became too few to be able to remember.

It is like that: a lessening of chances,
the thought that I will never again be in love
but will sit foolishly waiting for what is in the cards
while your face becomes a photograph, becomes
only a way I remember people looking.

Stephen Dunn

Building a Person

With the leftovers and etcetera of the poor
we can build a skeleton —
chicken bones and gruel (for glue) —
and perhaps the remains

of a slim cat on a skewer
for the spine.
Does anyone have a heart
for the heart we need

to give the skeleton feelings?
The hearts of the poor are always
too large or too shriveled,
but we believe a good heart

can be created. We are talking
about what appears extra
in this world
like those tongues

of the deaf and dumb
for texture and muscletone.
Hearts are rare these days (at the dump
we could only find a rib cage)

and sometimes we've needed a scalpel
to locate scruples.
Still, the poor make the best kind
of orphan and orphans will often

trade crucial parts of their bodies
for a home. Already, our skeleton
is looking more human, and the rich —
who pass by this vacant lot

where we are building — are interested.
They have donated the used parts

of their servants, even a brain
has come in from a downstairs maid

who (it was said) split open her head
by accident. They want a plaque made
and their names engraved and the plaque
affixed to the body. This, of course,

is not impossible. Old tin cans
from the poor's garbage could be flattened
and everyone, when it comes down
to bodies, is an amateur engraver.

Soon (as planned) the Missing Persons Squad
will stop by with folks
who have lost their loved ones.
The bidding will start.

The auctioneer will say: Remember,
it takes money to maintain a person.
And, as always, the same folks
will go home emptyhanded.

Stephen Dunning

Player

I see you, you're twelve
maybe thirteen, teasing two boys
before your band begins to play

and I watch you, for distance
as you count measures and hit drums
The tuba player turns and grins

because he likes you too
Who doesn't? You pop your eyes
and pucker up, smart aleck faces

Now you're thirty two
playful and naked, your hair
long and dark, your eyes

full of pizzazz. I grin
nibble on your shoulder bone
wishing this piece would never end

Now you're twenty one
your clown eyes frolic, your body
is ripe as a puddle

everything about you
fit as a fiddle: your gypsy hair and bones
and moves in perfect harmony

helping us hold the beat
make the most of the music
helping us keep time

Quinton Duval

I Point Out a Bird

for Nazim Hikmet

I don't know the species, but this one has been
a lot of places on this earth. Has been
in japan and bolivia and turkey too.
He must have seen the jungle when it was wet
with rain. The marketplace in wherever it is . . .
that old song says it, beautiful and alive, but
nothing like the slow song coming from its mouth.
I believe the eyes shine like that because
they are sad and have become polished from
constantly closing over tears.
The ivory beak, the jewel we find in all

animals, cracks enough to let the song escape.
  This bird I've seen before walking out
of the forest with its head down. Do you remember?
Riding a hot train, guns held over the head
to make more room. Hiding in a cart under a layer
of straw past guards, like a bottle of wine and
quite as fragile. Coming back home to an invisible
town and a wife made of clear air and smoke.

Absent Star

for my brother John

After you left, I took the green
marbles that were your eyes. Lying
there in a suit with no back. I thought
the strange silk touched your shoulders
and buttocks like women's underwear.
The sad shoes that looked fine but
split down the back, harelipped,
cheating my father.

Once I twisted your arm so hard
I swear I felt my own break.
The turkish moon I banged in your
forehead with a stone, has caught me
like an invisible hook and teases me
until I break down and cry.

The woman you married over
and over again lives on. She counts
the minutes like money and looks at me
as if to demand payment.
I do what you would have wanted:
Look away and name everything I see.
I shake my own hand and pretend
we are making up for good.

Richard Eberhart

Passage

Time as something concrete, like the wash of a wave
        Over a sea wall.
Is not time always coming on and over us?

Time! From the Leakey skull in the Rift Valley
        Has it not always been coming over us?

Not people, not events so much as time itself,
Abstract time as if not abstract, but concrete

Time! It rushed over us when we were striplings,
Over us in mid-life, over us in age.

Time the smacker without a grudge.
It is in the air surrounding my fingers,

It is in my mind in my skull,
It is in my legs walking and my voice talking,

Sightless time! What a sightless time we have.
We can't see it, but we feel it all the time.

Art Sinsabaugh

Frederick Eckman

Lullaby

What if, every time you walked, things
scattered before you, like ducks & drakes?

If I wrapped you in a quilt & gave you
to the gypsies, would you remember me long?

What if I made up a story about you & a tree
& candy hanging from the tree, & a funny hat?

If I did that, would you close those blue moons
of eyes? Would you go to sleep, go to sleep?

Aka

Depending on his mood & the hour of day,
the configuration of the sun & planets,
he is Jack the Ripper, Typhoid Mary,
Caligula, Genghis Khan, Crazy Horse,
or murderous little Charlie Manson.

Watching him through the front window
as he stretches out in a La-Z-Boy chair
you'd never know that he owns & operates
a castle full of costumes, dragons & weapons.
You see only that his hair is thin & patchy.

Seated at dinner forking in pot roast & carrots,
trotting across the lawn behind his Toro mower,
or at his desk neatly filling in Form G-7258-1
he may well be preparing to bloom at once into
Christ the King, Buddha, or great-peckered Zeus.

Cunning as an FBI man, polymorphous, innocent
as Adam wandering through the fruit orchard,
he wipes his bifocals on a single Kleenex tissue
& thinks: Helen of Troy, Camille, Bonnie Parker,
do I *really* want to go in drag on such a hot day?

W. D. Ehrhart

Money in the Bank

for Alfred Starr Hamilton

Sixty-one years
Of your life are gone and I
Have never heard of you
Until today.

I understand the poems
Simply grow
Beneath your pillow as you sleep
In your cheap boardinghouse room,
And you only have to rise
And type them in the morning,
Ten at a crack before lunch
And the daily paper you read
At the Montclair Public Library
Because you cannot afford your own,
Like the cigarettes
You pick up from the street.

Sixty-one years old,
And I have never heard of you
Because you are not taught in school
And your poems do not appear in *Poetry*
And your only book was not reviewed
Because we have no use for poets
Who have no use for us.

Well, Mr. Hamilton,
Now I have heard of you;
And tomorrow the mailman
Will give you this
(along perhaps with another summons
From the Garden State
Because they say you are a vagrant),
And you'll open it and find
Some person that you do not know
Has sent you money.

I'd like to say I sent you this
Because I simply care
About another human being.

But the truth is, Mr. Hamilton,
This money you receive
Is for myself,
And for the future;

And I send it out of fear.

Larry Eigner

After Shiki

Coming to see the cherries
he had his money-bags stolen

it's too bad

the man from the country

Unusual

moment

or animal
kept its curl the tail
waved
at the wind
on the branch up
as
the squirrel
stops
busy
some face and legs

The School Bus

retaining its sign
in the summer time
being useful, small

A Version of a Song of Failure

(By one of the Teton Sioux)
(After *The Winged Serpent,* Margot Astrov, p. 126)

s i n g i n g   a wolf
a   f a i l e d   m a n   in thought
I
was
now the owls hoot
at the fearful night

George P. Elliott

Sayer

Nowhere, on the way to the meaning,
straining to be in labor with yourself,
the word in your mouth *shit*:
sky bristling with mechanism,
contraption is mined from the sun
and towns powder your eyes:
reach to the midwife "teach me,"
who shrugs "teach you what?
fatherless cramp in the gut":
meadow too green, a graveyard,
grass preying on corpses,
stones the earth's knucklebones:
constipated with yourself, a fist;

in your ears "sapsucker, sapsucker,
changed your life yet, sapsucker?"
a mocker circling your crouch,
your mouth spits all over him,
he runs the way, abandoning:
slaked then, slack, spread-eagle,
frantic, panting for death,
encased in smear, untouchable:
but the rain comes,
uncontrived sky-fall softly
washing your voice to reach with:
not abrupt, as you'd thought, but groping,
half-awake and cockeyed, thirsty,
brains griping; somewhere:
poking around for the way,
false labor forgotten;
graveyards? those aren't headstones:
grass so green; corpses?
dig for them, all become flowers;
what way? so many the flowers:
that curled grandmother, her heart
shitty, spray her with words,
she'll sigh, she'll die at last:
that cripple there, flaunting the leg
he's pulled off, give him a word
to stick it on with, he'll talk:
comes the taunter "sapsucker, sapsucker,
given up already?" tell him
"I lost the way in a flower":
nevertheless, whatever else,
powder of mechanism drizzles,
towns gum people's eyes:
wash them daily with saying;
yet many seel, so many,
heads full of word-proof baffles:
they'll dare you to death if you let them,
spit your words into a ditch
by the way: *but here you are.*

Harley Elliott

For The Man Who Stole A Rose

Like everything else they
belong to the world at large
yet the bush gives a start

when your fingers ramble
in the blue twilight of May.

Grizzley bear in crepe sole shoes
sniffs the pink buds out
and takes one with a snap.
Now your nose hairs

shine with chlorophyll;
random atoms fill the air.
This entire constellation
of roses turns and looks.

The tenant in shadows
hears the teeth of green leaves tick
and you are caught red
handed in the roses
thief of roses favorite

flower of the brave.
Roses ladies hold against
their breasts wild roses
shaking in the rain you
make a getaway just as

the tenant reappears
with scissors and a
bottle of May wine.
Barefoot on the porch

he sees you dance through briars
a touch of wonder
rising in your skull.

Greg Field

Home Cooking Cafe

We are in Wieser, Idaho
Two young chicks
trot into the bus-depot-cafe
Three long-haired dudes
pitch pennies against its west wall
An old man puts a cheese sandwich together
Such is the entertainment

Edward Field

For Arthur Gregor

A child devoted to sacred study, pale,
his whole life this, and prayer, and ritual,
looked up one day and saw a butterfly,
went out and followed it, not knowing why,
through the ghetto shrouded in mystery and awe.
He climbed the walls surrounding it and saw
the world outside, and jumped without a thought
for those he left behind and what they taught:
that the life of play and foolish laughter is,
for all of that, no happier than his.
Without a choosing to or not to, he was out
and saw the hills, smelled hay, heard children shout,
and ran, his head uncovered, through fields of flowers
and fell in the grass and lay there overpowered.

Dennis Finnell

Working at a Service Station, I Think of Shinkichi Takahashi

Where once that flying red horse,
outlined in neon, revolved,
this sign now stands: Mobil.
I never believed in Pegasus
but the Company's version,
that winged horse, sold gas.

Here thistles spike up through
cracked asphalt, roots that finger
earth touch 6,000 gallon tanks
of Regular, Ethyl, No-lead.
There's plenty of emptiness here
yet no one seeks the Void.

But look, crows do flap lazily off,
stray dogs do piss on the thistles
and when a car pulls up a bell
rings and I say, "Fill 'er up?"

Art Sinsabaugh

Isabella Gardner

That Was Then

Union Pier Michigan. We called it Shapiro
Shangri La. People said I needed a passport.
I was the only Shicksa there Kolya Shura
Manya Tanya and Sonya, Sulya Myra and
Vera they were there. And Riva a young girl then.
Soda pop and ice cream parlors, no bars,
Delicatessens but no liquor stores.
They spoke fractured English fractured Yiddish
and fractured Russian when they did not want
their children to understand. Most husbands
drove down from Chicago fridays but mine
came to me thursdays bringing the squat green
bottles of Chilean white wine I drank
(he was angry if I forgot to buy
cucumbers) My daughter then five, now in
Bedlam, chased butterflies and thirty years
ago my infant son, now for some years
lost, was happy too. I washed his diapers
in a tub and hung them up in the sun.
Instead of a play-pen, my husband, Seymour,
called Simcha which means joy, made a paddock
for him. Dan did not like to be cooped up
(nor did Rose, my daughter Rosy; nor did she)
not then, not later, never. Dan was last
seen in Columbia South America.
Simcha little Rosy   littler Daniel
and the Shicksa we were all of us joy —
full then in Shapiro Shangri La when
we were young and laughing. On the lake beach
the women waded and grossiped. The men,
supine on the hot sand sucked in the sun
through every work and city tired pore
and on the blithe beach played chess needling each
other, "singing" they called it. The Shicksa
swam and her daughter, round pink Rosy made
castles out of sand and when the big rough
boys' unseeing feet crushed her battlements
she cried. (as she would later, as she did
later, as she does now and must again
in inexorable time) Ah but then

it was different. The first summer at our
Michigan Shangri La we shared one half
a cottage with Seymour's sister Molly
Molly the matriarch and my mother
too Molly ample Yiddishe mama
bountiful heart bountiful flesh married
to tender Ben Blevitsky book-binder
and Bolshevik, not Communist though he
thought he was and paid his Party dues.
He pressed on me, a bemused fellow traveller
The Daily Worker which I occasionally
scanned. Aside from Ben's misguided fealty
to a party that betrayed his each, his
every dream, he taught the Shicksa wisdom,
ancient, Hebraic, of the heart and pulse.
This Shicksa loved him all his life. He died
attacking Zionists. In the debate
the heckling struck his heart and aged eighty two
gentle Ben Blevitsky fell down and died.
That first summer the Shicksa shared the stove
with Molly who wouldn't let her cook
a meal but did teach her to cook kugel
and fix gefilte fish. (It was only
the Shicksa's second marriage and so she
had not yet lost her appetite for cooking,
that came after the fourth marriage when
she recklessly played house with a fifth man)
Political not pious there was not
kept, a kosher kitchen. Molly and Ben
once took the bus to Chicago saying
they'd be back saturday night for supper
saying Be well Bellotchka but don't cook!
Later Molly cheeks streaming with laughter
crowed to cronies "The Shicksa cooked a haser
for the Shabbas!" Stuck with cloves it was,
the scored cuts thumbed full of dark brown sugar
hot powdered mustard and the fresh squeezed juice
of sweet oranges and the whole ham smeared
with that luscious mixture and therewith glazed
and all ate that haser with high delight
the Blevitskys, Molly, Ben, and their Bob and Riva
Rose, Simcha and his Bellotchka — the cook
ate and ate while the infant Daniel slept.
That was then. That was then.

Dan Gerber

Love for Instance

Voices begin to flutter
like the wings of a frantic bird
so much to be said
the room will not hold them
so much talk of love
the word is finally a mouthful of dough
love love love love love
Now bang your head on your lover's knee
bang bang bang bang bang
and tell me
what's the difference

David Ghitelman

Grand Street & the Bowery

I see them go through the slums at night
towards an old age without silver
hair or grandchildren. Mornings I discover
them asleep on the sidewalk where the broken
glass of the bottles surrounds their bodies
like discarded halos. I only want
to forget their faces and the thirst
which flows through them, filled
with deaf cries, like an invisible river.

Chris Gilbert

philonous' paradox

not sure if he heard
when his friend was calling him
"he who doubts all things"

Robert Gibb

The Minotaur

She straddles me like this,
Her pelvis
A bowl I drink from,

Her legs the horns
Gleaming from my head.
Eyes shut it is almost

Like being born
And wanting to be alive
Like this forever:

Her body above me
Like the roof of a cave,
A maze suddenly centered

Where miles away
In the dark her hair
Reverberates with light.

Gary Gildner

Johann Gaertner (1793-1887)

In the blue winter of 1812
Johann Gaertner, a bag of bones,
followed Napoleon home.
He was cold; Napoleon,
riding ahead under a bear
wrap, fumed at the lice
in his hair. —From Moscow
to Borodino, from Borodino
to the Baltic Sea, Napoleon
fumed and slapped, and glared hard
at the gray shapes
pushing at his face.
And maybe ate a piece of fruit
he did not taste. If he
cried, we do not know it.
But Johann Gaertner, 19,
a draftee, a bag of bones,
blew on his fingers
and bit them, and kicked at his toes.
And chewed and chewed
a piece of pony gristle.
And once, trying to whistle
an old dog into his coat,
swallowed a tooth.
God save Johann!, Johann
Gaertner, 19, cried,
moving his two blue feet
through bloody holes his eyes
kept staring and staring at . . .
And in the midst of all this
one night God appeared, hoary and fat,
and yelled at him in Russian,
Kooshat! Kooshat!—
and Johann closed his eyes
waiting for one of his sharp white bones
to pierce his heart.
When none did, he dragged them
past the mirror Napoleon
gazed and gazed at his rasp-
berry-colored chin in . . .

and past windy St. Helena
where his former leader was already lost
among the washed-up herring.
And Johann kept going,
picking up crumbs like a sparrow!—
no longer hearing that tooth
grinding against his ribs,
but starting to feel the sun
on the back of his neck
for a change, and loving the itch
and salty wash of sweat
everywhere on his chest.
                                        And one day
holding up a jug of cool switchel,
he had swig upon swig upon swig
and felt his whole blessed mouth
turn ginger—
and he whispered a song
that came out *Ah, Johann . . .*
                        Thus,
having stopped, he stepped back
and took in his fields of hay,
his acres and acres of feed,
and his six black bulls
bulging against the sky.
And sitting down he ate
the giant mounds of sweet
red cabbage his ample wife
set before him,
and the pickled corn,
and the mashed potatoes dripping
galaxies of gizzards, hearts,
and juicy bits of wing,
and yet another slice
of her salt-rising bread
spread with his own
bee-sweetened butter.
(Often Johann stretched out big
in the clover, listening to his bees,
churn, churn, they said, *churn . . .*)
And praising God while licking his fingers
he allowed for a wedge of her
sour cream raisin pie,
and a mug of steaming

coffee out on the porch,
where he liked to stick his stockinged feet
among the fireflies,
and feel the slow closing
of his eyes . . .
                    And all of this
(including the hickory nut cake,
rhubarb wine, and the fine old fat-
bellied kitchen stove)
happened for many years
in little Festina, Iowa,—
where Anton Dvorak came to drink
local Bohemian beer
and hear the Turkey River;
and where rosy Johann Gaertner
dug down deep in the rich black dirt
to make his own hole
and one for his wife as well.

Tongue River Psalm

This is Tongue River, where lovers lie down,
where they bless the fox licking its fur in the bush,
where they play the rabbit's musical bones,
where they rattle two pebbles to praise the moon.

Robert Gillespie

When Both My Fathers Die

Like spirits that have wandered too far in a dream,
by morning surprised, by the highway awakened,
they have been standing along the white fence so long
the world has taken them for flowers.

When both my fathers die in the fall,
at Chicago O'Hare I watch the big jets lift from the sea
of roofs like dolphins in slow motion;
from above, the fir tips so kingly they've kept
the growth around them down.

When I think of prayers
the seasons ring me around with the obvious.
It is all chasms between stars,
the space between people.
The pips of bud on the sugar maple
become
the leaves flame,
the trees stand up soon
charred in their wood bones.

There must be one day when one is at the top of one's bent
balancing as if on knife blade.

Like a pike in a clear pool
the aircraft under us darts flat and dark green—
our shadow across the pine tops pulling ahead
into the Maine woods
as perfectly the image of itself
as a soul.

I feel my life coming in for a landing
like a large bird.

Fence posts vaguely this side of the lax pasture of mist,
the cowbell a buoy,
pines unfurling sails in fog,
firs with no bottom like icebergs—

I feel I am always on the edge of the world
about to wreck and go under
the white blossoms of the apple trees
wet to knee high.

Daniela Gioseffi

Buildings

In the cellars of old churches frightened mouths
mutter violent Bible stories
and in department store windows there are bones
for sale. They glitter whitely in the twilight
of lamposts pressed to a cold sky. Along the sidewalk I see myself pass in the eyes of buildings
I know that hidden in the bedrooms of the city
children are rehearsing love
as if it were a pastime.
I am thrilled by my own loneliness.

Malcolm Glass

Staying Ahead

Fire runs faster than emus, rams,
or 'roos across the outback scrub.
The bald landscape lies there
asking for it; and once the wind
and flame concur, a wall of hell
ten feet wide scrapes the pastures
and hills to cinder black.

"The worst thing you can do is run,"
Jack told us. "You'll end up trapped
or run down. You can drive back
through, if you have to. It's risky,
but if you're caught on the downwind
side of home, you have to chance it.
Turn up wind, floor it, heads down,
hold your breath, and pray. Chances
are you'll shoot right through."

"And if you're home and the fire
is moving your way, close up the house
and sit tight. The damn storm
of fire moves so fast it washes
right over the house. It's gone
before you realize it got to you.
The house will save you. It gets
a good blistering, but a good house
like this one—iron roof and stone—
will make it."

Like an ark, I thought.
But it wasn't until I got back home,
safe among the familiar trees,
the labelled streets and nameless
hills, back in the heavy green cover
of this land I was born to travel
from, that I realized how many times
I had walked out the back door
onto scorched ground—safe again.

—New South Wales/Tennessee, 1969

Patricia Goedicke

The Girl in the Foreign Movie

When she walks by — astonishing!
The small globes of her breasts don't fall
They rise, they are as firm as fruit

But better, sweeter, more delicious,
Prancing around in her skin she's a pony
Brushing her teeth, cutting her toenails

Her shaggy mane is a flag of curls
Lifting along her neck . . .

I tell you it is astonishing to see her:
The soft, triangular cunt hair
And the hairs on her head *match*,

Just as if it were perfectly natural
There she is, eating an apple on the screen,

Laughing and then talking
Very seriously, something about politics,

I suppose I should remember what but I forget,
After all those years in hiding

She makes me remember the moon
On the Snake River when I was thirteen,
Naked at midnight, in warm water

She makes me remember violets
And wild sweet strawberries, hidden

On a freckled hillside, in the sun
Among the sparse thighs of the grass

The wonderful tart flavor that was waiting for me
Under the stubby fingers of the leaves.

The Death Balloon

Most people simply ignore it, they have to,
From morning to night they are cheerful

And I also, except I have seen it
Once too often, hovering . . .

Even in my country
Wrinkled, fat
It floats over rivers and fields

Slack as a dirigible it hangs,
It casts a cigar shaped shadow . . .

I lie on my bed spread-eagled.

The red hot clinker of fear sizzles
Next to my collar-bone, my heart . . .

I have come unstuck from myself.

Am I a child, with soap
Foaming in its frightened mouth?

What we ignore by day
Returns to us by night.

Drinking dust, and choking
I lie down with Death,
I rise up with Death,
In life I am pregnant with Death . . .

Behind barbed wire the blackened,
Interminable cries of the dying.

But this is my body, it is mine
I say to myself,

If God — Oh
But what's He
To me? Nowadays

What's spirit but a flat tire?

Give me my own skull
And crossed-bones for a compass.

Wearing my oxygen mask for safety
I'll shovel Death, I'll wear it.

If I could hold your hand
And mean it,
If I could care . . . .

But no, nothing would change.

The Death Balloon is coming,
Escaped bubbles of gas crawl
Like maggots everywhere.

At the Center of Everything Which is Dying

You swear you are as healthy as the next person,
Like anyone else you despise pain,
At every election you are innocent of war

But inside you there's a swamp
That keeps pulling you towards it

Waiting for the next outbreak of the disease,
The next rifle shot, the explosion

Almost as if you had a secret lover
Faceless, waiting for you in a closet

You keep looking for it everywhere,
At board meetings, at every planning session

Sucking the possibility of catastrophe
As if it were a sore tooth

At the center of everything, which is dying
The ooze of pus attracts you:
Soldiers and chronic invalids

Have nothing to do but obey orders,
All the difficulties of life are done for them

As on a sickbed one forgets everything,
Centering on the self only

Even when the outside of the onion is pure
Gradually the soft spot, the delicious rot

Keeps seeping outwards,
From one layer to the next

Inside everyone it is possible there's a viciousness,
A lascivious finger beckoning

Pornographic as sex
Without love there's a stink
Inside everyone it is possible

There's a stagnant pool that wants to be fed
New bodies, every day.

At The Party

When everyone comes together
Fighting, excited
Each one for all the others,

Men, women, children
Their whole lives
In one room

Because it is a matter of electricity
Because it is a matter of love
That room will take off into the heavens
And fly.

And whether it goes up and up like a balloon
Losing all its people, here, there

Or whether it goes careening from pole to pole
        like a lost dove
Finally it is bound to bump into a mountain and give
One last performance:

Everyone will be standing up
With his arms around everyone else,

Ribbons of laughter will trail out
Over the tops of the trees,

Animals and skyscrapers will look up
Wondering,

For that room will be golden,
Lit up like a waffle
Throbbing above us like a comet

And always, everywhere
Someone will be waving from the window
Come on up, come on up.

Paul Goodman

THE MESSIAH-BLOWER

I have been given a horn and appointed to wait and blow it when the Messiah comes to our town. If I have been appointed? or have I appointed myself to this position? In any case I have a horn in my hand.

Naturally, from time to time, I cannot resist giving it an experimental toot. This makes a few (usually the same ones) prick up their ears and come running. But most people pay no attention to such a peep; they think, no doubt, that when the Messiah really comes, the sound will have a stirring unmistakeable appeal.

Really, with my tooting, I am trying to get a rise out of a person on the second floor there.

I am lying about those occasional toots. Actually I blow and blow my brains out. They are going to pass a decree to keep me off the streets.

Am I betraying my office by tooting at that second floor? But why shouldn't the Messiah come out of *that* window? If I don't rouse him, who will?

Questions. Questions. I whose vocation is for heart-easing hallelujahs, sound nothing but discordant blasts. Almost I could believe that the Messiah doesn't come just because I make such a damned racket! . . . Yet the Messiah will come anyway (I cannot prevent it either), and then shall I sound my heart-easing hallelujah.

March 1948

Rosalian 75

Arthur Gregor

At the Trough

Weary of the day, of small-
mindedness and petty manoeuverings,
I drove out toward the hills
and stopped near the fields
where sheep and cattle graze.
Hearing the birds from all sides
and seeing the animals, trees,

the hills in hazy distances
I soon felt refreshed, especially
as I watched the sheep marching up
to drink at the trough outside
the shed. What do they know —
I thought as they stood there
and drank — what do they know

when later in their sleep
they do not dream? Where are
they then? Where I am, when I,
like they, have left the day,
lie deeper than in dream
and drink; not I, not they
aware of our bodies then
but drink, drink, till I wake?

What comfort as I drove off
to think that when in the dark
inside their shed they sleep
drenched in an innocence
they at least need never leave,
and when I have gone to sleep
I am no different then,
no different then from them.

Horace Gregory

Siege at Stony Point

Three Voices Speaking

Birds, birds—birds, birds, birds—
A darkening of wings across the sky,
A half a million birds dropped from the air
Flying through sleep, through half-lit dawns and hours,
Black myrmidons in passage everywhere.
Starlings and crows, ferocious wrens,
Voracious hawks, and vultures drinking oil
Empty our lamps while foraging rooks
Deplete our fruits and strip the willows bare.

Some say, 'The birds are sent by Eskimos,
From antique Crees in Arctic wildernesses,
From stark Siberia, or Greenland's glassy waters,
From dark-skinned countries, fast in endless cold.'
Others insist that they took flight from County Clare
Straight up from fallen cottages, wrecked iron,
Moss-ridden stones, and broken angels
Lying among dank stubble and the thorn.
And ravens, fifty thousand strong and heady,
Are among the lot, their red eyes glaring.

Aristophanes once knew the birds as brothers,
He half implied this transient universe
Was theirs to wander, cherish, or remake—
The voluble Hoopoe, or raging parakeet—
But what of Earth?
                        that strange, elusive,
Far distant apparition of orange light,
Seen from a cockpit on the rim of outer space?
The gods may well desert it.
It is there for anyone to take.

Alvin Greenberg

sungrazer

and from what distances, to this, are we come
wringing our hands in the primal stuff of the universe
incredible density. such a spray of phenomena we are become

by whose wide surprising trail the world itself interprets
o tell me again the story of our elliptical beginnings
orbits crossed. the heavy gravity that dictates our turns

everywhere in this semi-legible scrawl, with you, i am
reading the close, deliberate inscription of the sun
far side emergence: evening. are we seen? is it done?

and those orbits to cross again: this one and this one . . .

so?

so: standing in the front yard in january in the evening
cold: i see nothing. nothing revealed as promised here
but because it's said the light will come and come again

around me, however gross and remarkable the times, i exist
like a monument to an historical event which hasn't yet
occurred. but will. o will. i *tell* you, friend . . .

does rumor have it one takes his cosmos too too seriously?
well, without i do so, it's got no meanings, eh?
or means itself. the same. is reflective, and bright

and *that* significance precedes us—me—through the night

Andrew Grossbardt

A River in Asia

somewhere to the east
a great river grows smooth
slowly calms itself

to the unnatural feel
of no boats creasing its surface
no bodies hiding from the long rays of light

and this stillness
this hush of water pushing down
only on water

settles like a song
on the dusk still burning
at the river's edge

over the fields swelling with new grain
on all the quick light bones
gathering at the river's edge

Daniel Halpern

Direction from Zulu

Be seated first thing upon awakening.
Nevermind the early hour. Dust the zinc
table, pull up your zebrawood chair —
this is zero hour: it's time
for zabaglione the Zionist next door
whipped-up for mornings like this.
Feed the animals that inhabit the zoo
your life has become.

The Zuni will bring buttered
zwieback and marinated zucchini

Your fingers with their many zircons are weightless
with the long night behind them, here
in this neutral zone that you have emerged from
out of the zodiacal night where the bull
lies down with the ram, the goat rides the crab
and the lion kisses so gently the virgin who balances
a scorpion on one breast, the archer's tattoo
on the other. In the pitcher of water beside you
the fish in his reflection is your twin,
seated beside you over the zinc table.

The zombie in the zoot suit you call your brother.
You are stony now.
You eat.

When the zinfandel loses its zip
look into the field, but do not be disturbed
when Zeus on his zebra zigzags into your field
of vision, takes out the zip gun, and provides
what will be your salvation.
This then is the final perfection of Zen.
In your zibeline robes remember this:

You are Zechariah. You are Zoroaster. You are Zebedee.

Mark Halperin

Concerning the Dead

Lined up single file, they make a point
which, though it has no weight,
sinks through the heart like lead.
None are angels: angels predate
the oldest. If these are parents, they have grown
used to the cries of their children
and are unmoved, indifferent;
they neither laugh nor rave. The thin
body of their voices seems to drone,
hovering just above
our warmer beds. They stare,
fouling our acts of love.

Alfred Starr Hamilton

Wheat Metropolis

Isn't this grinding the valves a little closer to your ears
Isn't this grinding the wheat that was noticed against the running board
Isn't this living a little nearer to the center of activity
Isn't this wonderful taking a car out west
Or taking a bus and all your elephantine belongings
And running as fast as your legs can carry you
Isn't this wonderful noticing the wheat against the windshield
Isn't this a yearling
Isn't this a slender reed
Isn't the corn a little green behind the ears
Isn't this a little affrighted
Isn't this daredeviltry of another kind
On a nickel or a dime
Or hitchhiking or nonetheless

Tom Hanna

Tree Poem on My Wife's Birthday

Distant Wisconsin
Trees bend desperate branches

Some old father elm
It wants you alone

You are twenty-seven
I will fill your belly now
My own winter tree

Here are the old hills
We make our home
Out of weathered boughs

I am picked up by the wind
My voice begins by the woods

I took your word
There is no love
Without leaves falling

Kenneth O. Hanson

Nikos Painting

He looks at the white square
accusingly. Blue.
Its need blue he says
seized by decision.

The blue paint goes down
his breath moves it around.

In the middle in the middle
he urges impatient.

Its need sun
its need moon

he says dancing
to Turkish music on the radio.
All they sing without teeths
how can sing without teeths?

I put white. (He puts white).
I put green. (He puts green).
Come on *come* on
he says to the canvas
Nikos loves you.

Donald Harington

The Villanelle

Regard the motion of the villanelle:
Its ins and outs and comely dips and sways.
A couple must unite to do it well.

The two of them will make a carrousel,
For dancing circles which are roundelays,
Around the motion of the villanelle.

They never touch until they bid farewell
And then they meet in passionate embrace.
A couple must embrace to do it well.

Impassioned in the dance's magic spell,
No single movement of a foot betrays
The comely motion of the villanelle.

Each step by step their movements parallel
And compliment the partner's dancing ways.
This couple must conspire to do it well.

The moment's coming when the rules impel
The dancers now to fuse in final phase:
Regard this motion of the villanelle:
Our couple have embraced and done it well.

Michael S. Harper

Mahalia

—a voice like hers comes along once a milennium'—MLK, Jr.

High-pitched waves of glory
bring you down in Chicago;
though satan should be bound
and it is spring
the death of him
inspired, dreamed
in glory to Memphis,
your choired practice
this spirit bowl-flesh
rouged echoing full faces
torn in shakes of saving—
her transcendent voice.

Words, sungstrewn, always the last word:
high-pitched, resonant
whole sister fortified in Jesus
here in these deathmarch horsedrawn
blessings: most hearty bedrocked
sister with bad heart weakening
our ecstatic pain:

and who is listening?
head-dressed high-pitched whole sister
in the choir-chariot down
who is listening to your name.

Cannon Arrested

for Julian 'Cannonball' Adderly

Somethin' Else and
Kind of Blue
bleed back to back
as the Cannon arrests,
his V-shaped heart
flowing in glycerine
compounds of fixed signs
stabilized in his going:
who helps him as he softshoes
starstreamed joculars across
each throated arch of song,
stylings of separation?

His fat silent reed
beds down in Gary,
shanked by Stevie Wonderful's
moment of silence,
these mosquito whinings
near the liter can of gas
I pour into Buick 59.

In some unmarked Floridian grave
another ancestor shakes
to your damnation,
her son perhaps pulling a giant
sailboat behind his Cadillac
to sporty Idlewild, Michigan,
sanctified in attitudes
of 'Dis Here' on this side of the road,
'Dat Dere' *going over* on that side,
and the boat docks before me
in distant transformed banks
of you transporting this evil
woman's song pianola-ed
on Interstate 80, cardiac bypass
road-turn you didn't make,
your fins sailing over boundaries,
lined fingerings in a reefered house,
a divided storehouse near a black
resort town, this sweet alto-man
wickered in vestibule, drifting away.

Stephen Harrigan

Over To God

A century of evening prayers
rises to the ozone. The shield
is breaking down, and the great
eyes behind it, watery now
and stung with happiness,
know nothing of the dangers
their gaze can cause us.
Pregnant rats too long in God's sight
develop cancer in their gloomy organs.
Does anyone doubt anymore
it is the same for us?
Yet in his loving ignorance
God cannot know this.
He is like the mother who believes
with all her heart that white bread
is good for her children.
So let the shield dissolve,
give over to God what we all know is his,
the molecular swarm of grace
that is so deadly
but so cruel to withhold.

Judy Ray

William Hathaway

Apology for E.H.

Oh, most natural grandson I was
to keep old skin at arm's length;
Stale breath in a polka-dot dress,
propped from car to chair on my strength.

It seemed you lived forever then, an Easter
fixture at the table's end, too old to chew
the ham, isolated, deaf and always bitter
that each year light dimmed and children grew.

From love and pain in your silent, blurry world
you jumped the gun with crisp hundred dollar bills,
searching each strange face for gratitude. We failed
you to the end, afraid of your fear, old woman smells.

Closer now, not from loss or virtue seen too late,
you swell my emptiness, materialize my fate.

Samuel Hazo

The Next Time You Were There

After Paris, every city's just
   another town.
            Elephants could roam
   the Metro, Marly's horses
   could invade the Tuileries, wishbone
   arches on the Seine could shatter
   under traffic, and Parisians could
   refuse to estivate in August . . .
Appearing every day in Paris
   would be Haussmann's Paris, still.
At home, you'd like to die the way
   you live in Paris, telescoping four
   days into three, feeling that your best
   is just ahead, protesting
   that you need more time, more time,
   protesting to the end.
                  And past

the end . . .
But you exaggerate.
This capitol you share with France
is just another web—somewhere
to breathe and board and be.
You bring there what you are,
and what you are is nowhere
any different.
This makes
the Trocodero just a penny's patch
of grass, the Place de la Concorde
a wide and spindled planisphere,
and St. Germain-de-Prés another
church.
Weathering your dreams,
bronze Paris of the doorknobs
turns into the turning stage
called here that stays the same
as everywhere right now.
On that
quick stage a man keeps happening.
From Paris to Paris to Paris
the only life he knows
is anywhere and always coming
true.
That man is you.

Tom Hennen

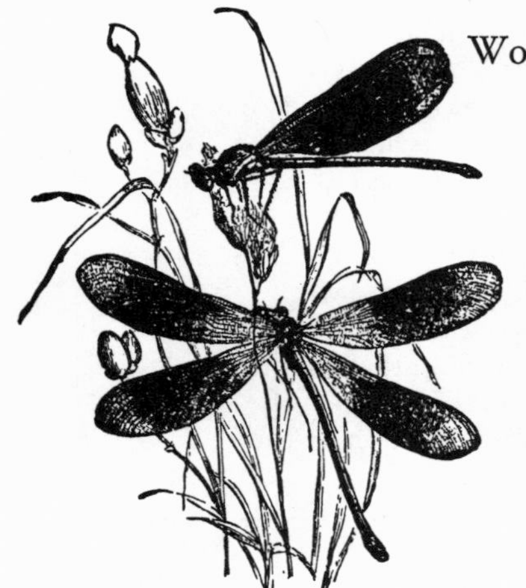

Working Near Lake Traverse

Reedy islands
Prehistoric green
Poke up
Through the haze.

If I stand still
Shadows gather near me.
From a distance
I look just like
That dark
Bunch of woods
Over there.

Unusual Things

East wind.
A straight line of spruce roaring
Louder than the rain.
I forget myself.
The field is inside me.
Not very intelligent
I now know an unusual thing:
    a beautiful rock just picked up
    wants privacy
    and can change
    to an ugly stone
    in the palm of your hand.

Usually An Old Female Is The Leader

Autumn has a mother.
Today
She's cold and wet.

A woman can draw heat
From a piece of furniture
Or a cloud.

A man
Can't get warm.
He tries to shoot down
The old hen duck
As she leads her flock away from snow.
His shotgun pulls him into the sky.

Ruth Herschberger

Watergate

McCord and Liddy and all those bums—
Men, men, men, men—
Questioning, answering, "doing"
And paid—how boring
On oh such a fine May day—
How boring to listen to Watergate—
Rather the Outlook, the sunny field,
The breath of air and the rocking chair
Outside my cabin door—
Than honoring all those winners and losers,
Those righteous men—
Can men be righteous?
Those righteous unrueful ruthless men
On a May day in Washington.

Yaddo

Whether to vegetate, or write with heart?
Expel the people at breakfast from one's mind?
Exclude the shared bathroom, and the waiting lunch?
Forget the smell of chicken in the mansion
Hall, not reminisce of bacon, waited-on,
The privilege of wealth and genius, us?
No, we must think of grass blades
And the roaring grate; must ponder the imponderables
Of spring; see May as symbol only,
Green on the page; whet appetite
For words, and birds, not apples
On the tongue, nor roast in the gut.

Geof Hewitt

Chickens

And aren't those baby chicks
creatures of my acquiescence
letting a particularly broody banty hen
have some eggs to set?

Now she acts as if they're completely her
creation, even the rooster has to sneak
blessings to his heirs, and I
get pecked for coming near.

Those chicks get down under her belly
and stay warm in that darkness,
sputtling over each other in morning
when I remove the raincoat

from their cage, the limits of their world
so far. I make their day begin
by letting sunlight in, and feed & water them,
they peek out from underneath

their banty's feathered gut and peep:
"Hey that's Him! I saw God's hand unveiling day!"
And I sit here, twelve hours later, August 26
8:30 P.M. and already now the sun is down

Yeah, Winter's coming
darkness—God!—I hate to see it come.

Ben Plays Hide & Seek in the Deep Woods

Don't hide too far Geof
Or I'll have to find you all over the place

Jeanne Hill

Lines from a Misplaced Person

hawthorn apples turn red years stumble
into shaggy humpbacked clouds
Buffalo Buffalo
what hast thou wrought?
smoke of steel
where is the sun?
I develop the eyes of a mole
and the Black Rock Canal bleeds in my skin

Pati Hill

Time was
when all you had to do was
carve a rose out of stone
and the world stopped

(thorns and petals grew more
than willingly from the same
stem)
If you wanted to know how the cathedral
was progressing
you could walk into the forest
and look into the hole
the stones came out of

No one works in quarries now

Our mountains are made of paper
and the smell of thyme and lavender
has disappeared

Some of us still believe
in our own creating
but hardly anyone feels
he has to be equal to his own fate

Two lovers sitting on a tomb
peeled an orange and ate the rind

Three lovers in a cosy room
slept with arms and legs entwined

Four lovers on a dusty road
looked for God and found a toad

One lover in a rented flat
wrote his name and that was that

How many lovers does it take
to weave a sweater from a snake?

On the beach
a big dog lies
one side staved in
like some romantic freighter
or a snug harbor for hatching fish

My little girl cries
Catch me, Mama!

Her footprints fill with water
almost before she leaves them
and the day flutters out like

a bolt of blue cambric
freshly escaped from the drygoods factory
across the bay

Michael Hogan

December 18, 1975

You meet your father after nine years.
At least that's who they say he is.
So you look for something in the eyes or mouth,
you speak quietly putting him at ease.
Everyone thinks this visit is important.
But they don't know about the dream.
They don't know that you are in the dream
and also the one dreaming.
He hugs you and that seems important,
so you hug him back.
You know there should be something
familiar in all this.
You are a boy embracing your father.
You are that same boy watching yourself
embrace your father.
To think that somewhere nine years ago
you did this in the same way,
doesn't make it more real.
Still, it is difficult to leave at the end
and, even when the guard comes and the chairs are pulled back,
you do not awaken.

Survivors

Last night there was a storm in Tucson:
trees launched into blackness, roofs leaping
from the startled cubes of houses.

A battered sparrow, winded,
but with nothing broken by the storm,
has come to rest on this sliver of grass between cellblocks.

Survivors know it is chiefly a matter of luck.
Being in the wrong place at the right time
we rest together
gathering strength for flight.

Jonathan Holden

December Sunset

This last soft lie. Almost
inaudible. A tenderness.
This lingering look. Ambiguous.
As if beckoning us. The road
already lonely. The birch trees
flushed. Fierce. All facing
west. Waiting. In suspense.
A few lucky twigs. Still
blessed. A few shingles
grazed. A faintest
remembrance of kisses across
the barn roof. Sighs
of light over the sleek
drifts. A few wisps of it
left. A breath of it.
Along the fence rail, a last
rare whisper. And less. And
less. And less . . .

Anselm Hollo

The Caterpillar

w/ round black eyes

big & furry it goes
through the gate i built

& it is LOOKING AT ME
on its way down
                    down down

2 years old i am
& surely
    surely it is so

1936

After Verlaine

right now it is raining in Iowa City
        but it ain't rainin in my heart
                nor on my head
                because my head
        it wears a big floppy heart ha-ha
                    it wears a big floppy heart

*   *   *

vibrant mutants of the future
        i love you

but what can you do with this love
or a twentieth century fossil

        well anyway
i love you to bring you about
that is what love is all about

Jim Howard

Newspaper Hats

They are no substitutes for gas masks
Or lead helmets. But you can shape them
any way you want yourself. Here is one:

the Bishop's hat, and maybe if you make up
a prayer in your head, this one will funnel it up
and save something. Fold this here

and back over, tuck it in: the soldier's dress cap.
The headlines might rub off in your hair,
but that would be part of the job. Unfolding,

back to the original triangle hat—when the sun
blasts through what was an atmosphere, the brim
could provide a brief shade. I had a friend

who taught me these. He lives two states west now,
under the shadow of a mountain on giant shock absorbers,
a hollowed-out mountain no one climbs. Uniforms

with men in them go about their business there,
driving dark trucks over fluorescent streets
underground. Their families pass the food

and talk sometimes at dinner. The way they look
at each other is a story. I sit tonight,
give instructions to no one but the room,

and make newspaper hats for those people, for a friend
I had, for myself. And I try them on, hoping to see
how we wear the things that happen in the world.

JIM HOWARD

94

Boy Trash Picker

Why don't it come to the top
up here where I can get it.
Maybe a thing for me
to put over my bones.

Why's this barrel suck me down
in a belly like a sickfish's.
My old man arms rust & stay dark.

Why don't it come to the top here,
maybe an old shoe for my good foot—

I'd hop all the way down the next long block.

Lewis W. Hine

Richard Hugo

Cataldo Mission

for Jim & Lois

We come here tourist on a bad sky day,
warm milk at 15,000 and the swamp across
the freeway blinding white. No theory
to explain the lack of saint, torn tapestry.
Pews seem built for pygmies, and a drunk
once damned mosquitoes from the pulpit,
raging red with Bible and imagined plague.
Their spirits buoyed, pioneers left running
for the nothing certain nowhere west.
Somewhere, say where Ritzville is, they would
remember these crass pillars lovely
and a moving sermon they had never heard.

More's bad here than just the sky. The valley
we came in on: Mullan. Wallace. Jokes
about the whores. Kellogg and, without salvation,
Smelterville. A stream so slate with crap
the name pollutes the world. Man will die again
to do this to his soul. And over the next hill
he never crosses, promises: love, grass,
a white cathedral, glandular revival
and a new trout, three tall dorsal fins.

We exit from the mission, blind. The haze
still hangs amplifying glare until
two centuries of immigrants in tears
seem natural as rain. The hex is on.
The freeway covers arrows, and the swamp
a spear with feathers meaning stop.
This dry pale day, cars below crawl thirsty,
500 miles to go before the nation quits.

With Kathy At Wisdom

I only dreamed that high cliff we were on
overlooking Wisdom and the Big Hole drain.
I dreamed us high enough to not see men,
dreamed old land behind us better left
and we were vagabond.

We went twice to Wisdom, not in dream.
Once in day, odd couple after Brooks,
and then at night, dark derelicts
obsessed with fake
false fronts for tourists and the empty church.

I dream the cliff again. Evening. Deep
beneath, Wisdom turning lights on. Neon flakes
are planets when we touch.
I wake up shouting, Wisdom's not that much,
and sweating. Wisdom never will be bright.

Lord, we need sun. We need moon. Fern
and mercy. Form and dream destroyed.
Need the cliff torn down. To hold hands
and stare down the raw void of the day.
Be my contraband.

Three fat Eastern Brook a night, that's
my private limit. The cliff broke
and wind pours in on Wisdom
leaving false fronts really what they seem.
Morning Wisdom, Kathy. It is no dream.

Lewis Hyde

Ants

It is springtime and the ants come into the house.
They are searching for something, not in lines yet
but scattered all over as if a great wealth had been
changed into pennies and thrown about the room.
This is how it feels to be lost in a long depression.
They stick to what's what. They feel every surface
with feelers, like hands searching dressers in the dark.
Small and full of legs they crawl below the oceans of air
that smell of lilacs and roses, and do not get involved.

Wang Hui-Ming

Why I Carve These Poems

Reading poetry to me is like taking a solitary walk on a forgotten trail. There are moss-covered rocks to slip over and hidden mud puddles to step into, but these sudden jerks of body and the sensuous touch of the mud are the necessary ingredients of the total enjoyment. If some readers find these poems in wood hard to read, it is because I want to fill my pages visually with poetic rocks and puddles so that you have to slow down to read the poems carefully. There is no intent to achieve typographical niceties.

Woodcuts by Wang Hui-Ming
Poems by Robert Bly
Joseph Bruchac
Marilyn Chin
Madeline DeFrees
Robert Francis
Gary Gildner
Etheridge Knight
David Lattimore
Howard Nelson
Raymond R. Patterson
Fran Quinn
David Ray
R. Stephen Russell
William Stafford
Robert Stewart
Lucien Stryk
John Tagliabue
James Tate
Wang Hui-Ming

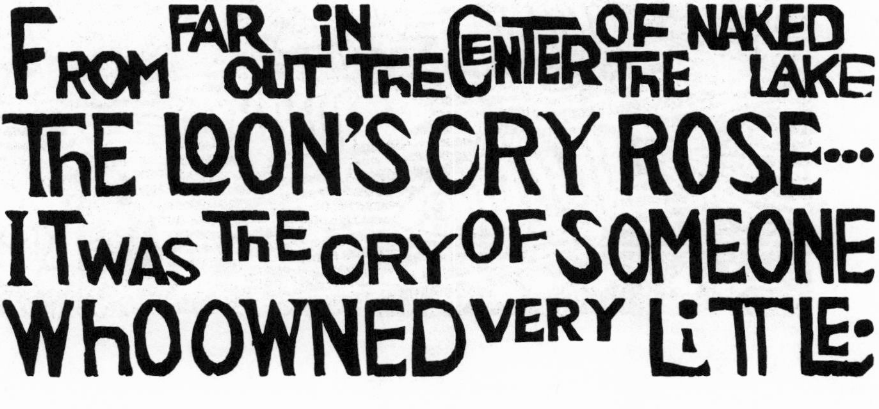

FROM FAR OUT IN THE CENTER OF THE NAKED LAKE
THE LOON'S CRY ROSE...
IT WAS THE CRY OF SOMEONE
WHO OWNED VERY LITTLE:

燕尾点波
绿皱
swallow follows
the curve of the sea
almost touching my hand
morning sun on the rocks
...Joseph Bruchac...
WANG

No dreams befall my pillow
tonight, except the dream
of Dawn, the blue unicorn
carrying me away
on her small back.
~Marilyn Chin~

WHERE THE HORSE TAKES WING
I GO ALONG, RIDING
THE SHADOW SIDE SADDLE
TO THE NEXT SPRING•
Madeline
DeFrees

AFTER THE AGE OF BIRDS THE AGE
OF INSECTS—THEIR INSISTENT WINGS.
ROBERT FRANCIS

In the Social Security Office

A widow rises
and steps forward
as if called upon
to say her sums --
as her legs are blue plums.
The knuckles on her handbag shine.

Poem by Gary Gildner · MW

Vigo County
Beyond the brown fields,
Above the silent cedars,
Black birds flee April rains.
ETHRIDGE
• KNIGHT

OUR HOUSE? NO IT'S THE
FIELDMOUSE'S WHO TAKES THE RENT
IN BUTTERY CRUMBS
DAVID
LATTIMORE

If My Wife Dies
If my wife dies, I will not mourn
because she has died, but because
she has just gone, and will be long
in coming again, with me in her arms.
~ Howard Nelson ~
WNG
AG

What is it like
But itself
--This day,
My life?
--Raymond R. Patterson--
WNAG

THE
CATARACT
FRAN
QUINN
ALLOWS
NO CONVERSATION,
IT LECTURES
EVERYTHING.

COBALT

COBALT WOULDN'T
LEAP OUT TO JOIN
THE BOMB • NOT
THE COBALT OF
THIS BLUE MING
VASE • NOT THE COBALT
OF A BLUEJAY • NOT
THE COBALT OF
YOUR EYES • MY LOVE

PAUL KLEE
EMBRACE,
1939,
SOMETHING SAD
ABOUT THAT
DAVID
RAY

SOMEWHERE INSIDE ME
A MOTH BURNS
R•STEPHEN RUSSELL•
IN FLAME ITS FLICKER ACROSS THE CEILING.

A WALK IN SEPTEMBER
WIL
LIAM
STAF
FORD
EARLY SNOW FALLS THROUGH
THE ORCHARD LIMBS PRETENDING
TO BE LATE BLOSSMS
WANG

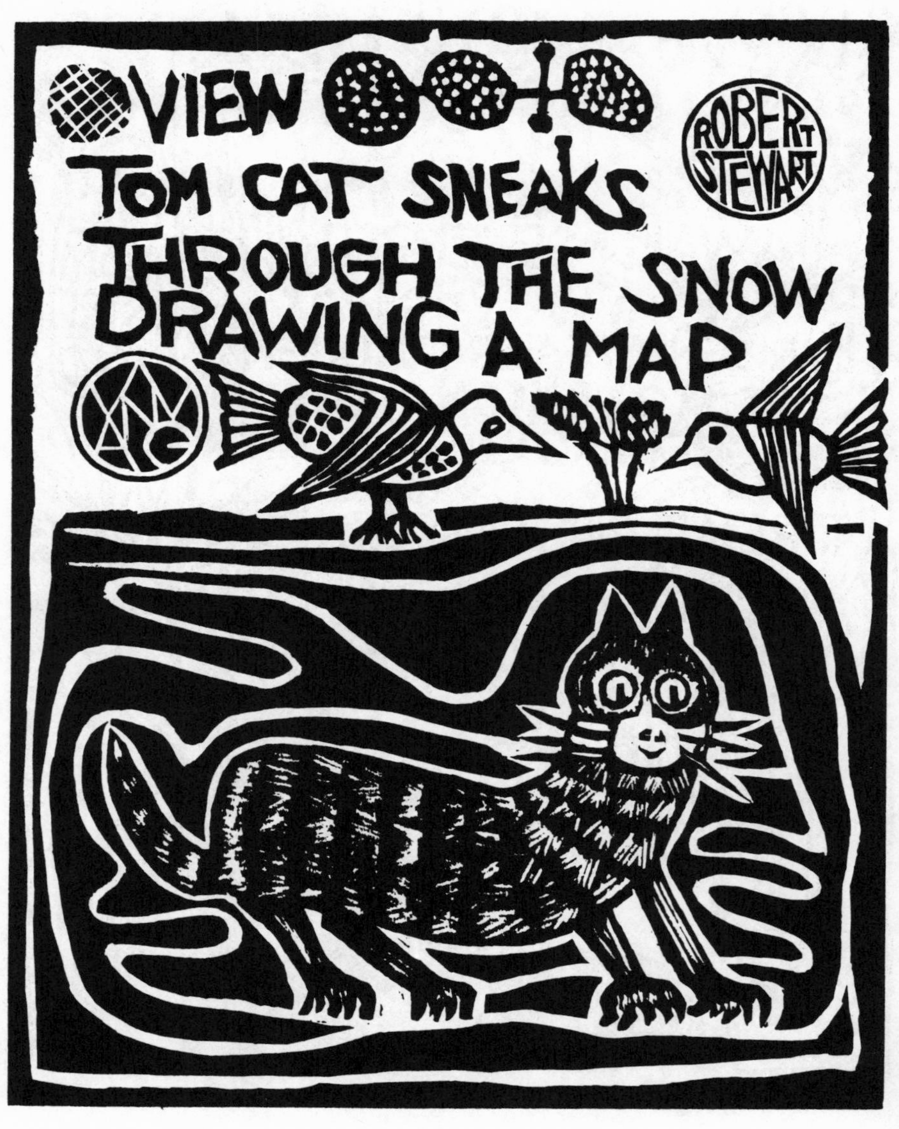
VIEW
TOM CAT SNEAKS
THROUGH THE SNOW
DRAWING A MAP
ROBERT STEWART

STORM
THE GREEN HORSE OF THE TREE
BUCKS IN THE WIND
AS LIGHTNING HITS BEYOND •
WE WILL RIDE IT OUT TOGETHER,
OR TOGETHER FALL •
WANG
LUCIEN STRYK

JOHN·
TAGLIA
BUE
PRIVILEGE
WILD
WORD'S
THE
WAS
TRUTH
FLOWERY
THE
TO
LADDER
THE
UP
GOING

SLOOPS IN THE BAY
WNAG
The sloops in the bay are talking in a little bottle language
language their laughter
is the most difficult number in the book,
a sweeping, a rolling
like the bilious voyage of sleep—
They are starting to burn
like the yellow leaves at the bottom of a dream.
They can't sleep now, it would be quite impossible.
Whispering like a garden of secrets.
James Tate

WINTER VIEW

IN WINTER THERE IS NO LINE
BETWEEN THE SKY AND THE FIELD.
SNOW ON THE GROUND AND HILLS
LIKE MOTHER-OF-PEARL INLAID
ON AN OLD CHINESE SCREEN. GREY
IN COLOR AND GREY IN LIGHT,
GREY NEAR AND GREY FAR.
IS THIS THE GREY ON THE SHINGLES
OF SEASHORE HOUSES IN NEW ENGLAND,
THE GREY OF ASHES ON A COLD HEARTH,
OR JUST THE GREY OF VISION, GREYING
WITH --- TIME AND THE DIMINISHING
EYESIGHT OF AN ARTIST?

去
赤裸々而
赤裸裸而来
POSSESS NOTHING • OWN NONE •
NAKEDLY COME • NAKEDLY GO •
WANG • HUI-MING

David Ignatow

With the Sun's Fire

Are you a horror?
Do you have eyes peering at you
from within at the back of your skull
as you look out in front,
managing to act perfectly calm
and self possessed, while knowing
you are being watched by a stranger
who without your consent
or prior knowledge examines your acts
of kindness and largesse to make you
feel an emptiness therein?

Those eyes are hollowed, polished bone.
Be well, I am seated beside you,
planning a day's work.
We are contending with the stuff
of stones and stars, with water,
air, with dirt, with food
and with the sun's fire.

A Time of Night

My mouth to utter a cry
that would have the street fall silent
and traffic halt, in despair with itself.
No such luck. No one will jump
into my grave. You keep reading this
with curiosity. We are in the world
dying together but scanning these words
you see me die alone.

Look up
and study those who to themselves
are persons, to everyone else
a time of morning,
a time of night.

Thoughts

Smash myself against a wall
to feel how deeply I love life
as I die in protest
at the silence in routine work
to keep a house.

Silent house,
its anguish stilled in bed
under covers in the night
of no history and no memory.
Night without appetite,
zero night, ringing ears
listening to silence of no future.
Night of fixation on death,
seeking it like sex,
pursuing it awake and in dreams
and token deeds to bring it on—
and then laughter of a pepsi cola kid
outside who howls his adolescence,
smashes his bottle on the curb.
I laugh. He is in my company,
with the first smashed bottle.

Threnody

Mother, in my unwanted suffering, I turn to you
who knew suffering like an odor of food
and breathed it in with that familiarity.
I can learn from you to become my self,
eating my sorrow with my bread
and gazing frankly at the world
as a man, as you a woman taught me
by your silence and acceptance of sorrow
as the bread itself.

Colette Inez

Qua Song

Qua qua qua
said the latinate duck.
Quidnunc Quintillian
never said fuck.
Quorum, questor,
buttocks qua ass
the concupiscent Teutons
pinched as they passed
muster in the fens
where conquering Romans
sorting out omens
pissed in the grass;
herbus verdus
going to hay,
good for a roll
with a qua qua maid
half dumb Vandal,
half wild Dane.

Crucial Stew

Crucial, that's me mother's word;
"this is a crucial election"

Christ's been banged
on the crucial with niles,
it were a bloody saight.

"Giscard d'Estaing represents
our highest aspiration,"
me mother writes,

she what
dumped me in an orphanage
in Beljum

is very neat about er person
and as been corresponding

with an English nicetype
for 23 years;
they ain't ever met.

Crucial, Comrade Crucial.
Communist atheist and Kulak killer,
she'd ave said of im.

We're two tough ducks, me and me mum,
she what dumped me with the Catolick Sisters.

Still, crucial, the word, seems a bit
thick and damn the bloody Pope
if I care what wins.

I lost me mother from the start
when they had me stabbing mutton fat
in that groveling pit
of highest aspirations.
Not an eyetheist in saight
but plenty of crucials with niles.

We was very neat about our persons.

Charles Itzin

Malcom, Iowa

Carrot headed boys,
their faces going out
of style, scatter
like beer cans,

The picnic tables,
pumphandles, lightbulbs
disappear, fathers,
holding down the county
in their hands like nails,
lock up the town
before them.

In the silence
of those terrible rooms,
the relics of generals and kings
still abdicate

Josephine Jacobsen

For Murasaki

Chrysanthemums
   come in spring too, now.
Force, again.

Unforced, their theme
   is autumn crisis:
wet winds, cold sun;

summer's colored
   death; the spicy
scent of fear, coming.

Amethyst, sun-yellow, bronze
   chrysanthemums:
the big chilly heads

crisp and taut
   curl to the center
tighter and tighter;

Or—small and stained, on
   earth-spattered sprays—
retain elegance.

Lashed to a poem
   like a petalled gloss,
they spoke for princes;

sprung from deep bowls
   at dusk in Paris
under the ruby lamp-fringe:

send, forth and back,
   in dumb color and scent,
Odette to Genji—

the chrysanthemum word.

Power Failure

The hard changes: concrete cracks and sprouts,
bull-dozers eat their spinach and grow strong.
Asphalt's black-plague ravages
where rubbish trucks cry, Bring out your dead!

Hastily the movie-theater buries
its faces and gestures in the parking-lot.
Six days alter the skyline. Five years build a stranger.
The manufactured blinds a frantic eye.

The pliant stays. The mango hangs itself
with fruity flowers and flowery fruit.
The tide runs very fast up over the rocks
making its sound of silk ripped,

and the sand blackens under the tide's shadow,
shines, pales before the tide comes back.
The oblique bat hunts down the lanes of dusk;
deep rainy valleys take the dark.

Last night the power failed. Below the moon
an Arawak, called back, could smell the island:
wind in its fronds; spice. And recognize its strong
shape under the gathered stars.

Dan Jaffe

This One is About the Others

In the kosher meat market
the piglet cried, "Love Me!"
A few frantic eyes,
a few snickers.
Of course no one hurt him,
But no one took him home to dinner either.

Who?

Who lingers always when the dream has blanched?
Whose off beat mutters know the basest flesh?
Whose wails are joy in the silence of the heart?
Who blows the hottest vibraharp of all?
Who swings spirals of song 'round even the bird?
Who is the source of soul?

ADONAI

Thomas Johnson

The Best Dance Hall in Iuka, Mississippi

Nothing's too good for the women
Of the Klan.
One by one
The records slot and spin

As they fan out over the dance floor
Like flies
On a bull pile,

Unaware that cut three to one
With the sawdust
Under their heels

Is that disappearance in shantytown
Of a young girl

From which their husbands
Have ground
Their complicity

To a fine, squaredance grit
Of powdered tooth
And bonemeal.

Richard Jones

Three Car Poems

I

A merry car
America
Merry car

Poor trait
portrait
Of blind
Billion volt
Fireflies

Methane mythed
Narcosis
Faster than a speeding locomotive

Gloomy luminescence
looming essence
Less

II

This yellow car
Was followed by
A blue car
Followed by a green one
Behind it a convertible
(Top up)
And a gray one
Old broken headlited one
(Right light)
Followed by a
New one
And another other
Blue one
(Isn't this fun)
Counting all the
Races of carkind
Formed in line
at a stop
Light

III

It was like the
Day when you
First roll down
The merry car's
Widowed windows

Space and airlight
Come inside outside inside
The merry car
And springs our
Winterly shell
Compartment uterus
And it all seems
So new to us
Having outside inside again

If you read this again
The left frontal lobe
in your brain will die
(½ a brain)

William Joyce

Small Town

All the clitorises are safely
anchored with rings
of green gossip. Too shallow
to steer a boat, I can only stare
at the Susquehanna River.
I have no one to talk to.
Yes, I have the children.
Parents send me the panaceas
for their bolted doors, the fabulous
innocence restored in the penumbra
of shopping carts, nearly squelched lives.
They say, "Help our Dick and Jane
to smile better with words
we have forgotten."
All day the children and I practice
the wolf's howl on arctic floors
as solid as shopping malls.
And each day I send them back
to their parents, their snouts
a little more pointed.
When the mothers hear, the once safe
clitorises shake like turkey wattles
in the shadow of my grate. At night
I teach this forsaken town to howl.

Arno Karlen

Bury Me in America

My grandfathers prayed
in Minsk and Kiev:
Put a fist of Israel's
soil in my grave, I want
to be buried at home.

I study their portraits, and
on a scratchy Thirties
record Lebedev sings from
New York, *Rumania, Rumania*

iz mayn sheyne heym — my
lovely home. Seranading
one exile from another,
a land where drunken peasants
sewed live cats in Jewish
women's bellies. Like my
mother, he made memory and
forgetting one melodious art.
I drank her tales of "home"—
White Steeple to the Russians,
for their church, to Jews
The Black Inferno, for pogroms.
Together we fondled her one
memory of it, Cossack boots
upon the floor above, while
she shivered in a secret
earthen cellar, smothering
as my bubba choked her cries.
And I, exile at heart, the
only Jewboy on the block,
only poet in the class,
dreamed her childhood
exile was my home.

But it was here I struggled
to become a friend, a lover,
husband, father, artist:
sweated language into
magazines and went to bed
begging angels to kiss my
mouth awake in poems;
hitchhiked past Ohio's
stubbled fields, past yellow
propane torches marching
drunken through Donora
to Monessen, read Gide by
the flames of slagheaps,
half-read Turgenev sitting
on a suitcase at a lamplit
crossroads, dreaming of a
redhead truckstop waitress
with thighs of doughy comfort;
savored The Village's sour
summer dawns after love with

crazy strangers; watched a
son born and gaped tear-blind
in the snow; fought my first
fight, when someone called me
Dirty Jew. This is my
sheyne heym, sweet home.

If lucky, wise, and brave,
we earn our deaths instead
of falling by mad lottery.
Films of dozers burying
Buchenwald's slippery heaps
of twig-limbs, skulls, and rags.
Those could be my own sweet sons.
I weep in rage, in grief,
knowing half the world
still wants to bury us.
Alive and lucky, first among
my clan to scorn bar mitzvah,
now I lead the family seder:
I want ceremony for my sons—
all poets, all believers,
know form is meaning even
in this fractured land.
The heart feeds more on
usage than on sudden
passions, and children
of exile must make
homelessness a home.

War in Israel, dust and
thunder piling over Sinai.
I prepare to volunteer,
praying: If I die there,
put a fist of America
in my grave, I want
to be buried at home.

Dave Kelly

The Day the Beatles Lost One
To the Flesh-Eating Horse

Cold rain, a steady wind, March is leaving us in one of her two styles. The room I am sitting in is not well heated; I wrap myself in sweaters and blankets. I look through the window. The flesh-eating horse is finishing the carcass of a dog he dragged in last night. He looks up at me and whinnies, his teeth streaked with victim's blood. This afternoon we will ride to town for the evening paper. There will be nods of acknowledgement, a large glass of whiskey at the local bar for me, the arm of an accident victim for him. He knows this and is happy in the knowing. At this moment, though, I am busy writing a letter to the editors of the newspaper we subscribe to here.

It is a paper published in the city twenty miles away. In the letter, I am explaining the absolute need for a third world war, to clear the air, I explain, to flush the rust from everyone's blood. Meanwhile, the piano tuner downstairs breaks into a flourish of dawn to announce that he has completed perfecting our upright, a fine instrument, over seventy years old, that had nearly lost a battle with nests of mice. He is playing that love was such an easy game to play but that he believes in yesterday. He wants seventy-seven dollars and fifty-five cents for making the piano capable of this song. First I sit down to the piano, but the piano is no longer capable of dawn or easy games to play.

Angry, I look up at the tuner. He tries to explain something but I am no longer interested. I lead him out to the yard. Then, back upstairs, I return to my letter to the editors. "Another world war," I write, "to clear the air and clean the blood." Then I smile. Another war and more piano tuners for my horse.

Fall Letter

All day long I have been trying
to put myself into the middle of this:
Pain, a sort of terror and the desire to sleep away
the whole afternoon.

Each year I have teeth taken away from me,
hair and assurances that I am loved
by friends or family. At night,
almost forty, I suffer from insults I received
in high school: Lois who said she wouldn't go to a worm-fight

with me, Faye who would, the coaches
who left me on the bench all season.

I grow fat, I lose weight, I grow fat again.

October is coming, the room
is filled with flies. The children
wear their new school clothes,
the youngest wears the oldest's dresses.

They sing together about teachers and books,
about the rain, rain, going away.

They go away and are asked about the number ten
or the name of the place Lief Erickson sailed from. I
read them William Carlos Williams and they look
from me to the television set.

The phone woke me this morning and I
was in a rage all day. I shouted at my wife,
struck my youngest daughter
and tied the dog outside in the rain. When
he howled I went out and kicked him.

Finally I stomped upstairs like a sick bear and took a nap.
The nap took the rest of the afternoon. Now,
although I'm still tired, I can finally smile.

Listen,
when you come to visit us and the weather changes
I have a sweater you can borrow,
it will fit you, I

keep it for that. The children
are throwing a ball, they are in the field

under my window. I am awake and smiling. They
all have new jackets. November is coming
and all the flies will soon be dead.

Then I will be sane again, I will
sit in a room free of flies and write superbly of snow.

David Kherdian

Uncle Jack

Jack, that nurse at the Veteran's
Hospital must have been interested
in more than your loving, because
the story that preceded you home
said you went out and bought a
pistol, loaded it, aimed it at
your foot, and said: One more
step in that direction and I'll
see to it you never walk again.
We enjoyed that story all the years of
your life—your witty, sad, funny,
beleaguered life. You didn't have
a drop of luck, and I believe in
the cosmic balance of things, that
you were put here to pass between
and among others, your life less
your own than a possession to be
shared. We borrowed bit by bit,
until your borrowed life was gone.

Melkon

Father I have your rug.
I sit on it now—not as you
did, but on a chair before
a table, and write.

It is all that is left of
Adana, of us, of what we
share in this life, in
your death.

In my nomadic head I carry all
the things of my life.
And on certain distant nights,
I take them one by one.
And count.
And place them on your rug.

IRENE MAC DONALD

Lewis Carroll

Galway Kinnell

Brother of My Heart

For Etheridge Knight

Brother of my heart,
don't you know there's only one
walking into the light, only one,
before this light
flashes out, before this bravest knight
crashes his black bones into the earth?

You will not come back among us
to amaze our world into your songs again,
your cried-out, laughing face
the same, touched by a pure, purgatorial glory:
those who die by the desire to die
may love their way back,
but as moles or worms, who only want
to grub into the first sorrow and lie there.

Therefore, as you are,
this once, this lifetime only, in this world
where you will not go on singing forever,
sing, even if you cry, the braveness
of the crying turns it into the true song—soul brother
in heaven, on earth
broken heart brother,
sing to us, here,
in this place that loses its brothers,
in this emptiness only the singing sometimes almost fills.

Etheridge Knight

We Free Singers Be

If we didn't have the music, dancers
would/be soldiers too, holding guns
in their arms, instead of each/other.
—Fr. Boniface Hardin

We free singers be
sometimes swimming in the music,
like porpoises playing in the sea.
We free singers be
come agitators at times, be
come eagles circling the sun,
hurling stones at hunters, be
come scavengers cracking eggs
in the palm our hands.
(Remember, oh, do you remember
the days of the raging fires
when I clenched my teeth
in my sleep and refused to speak
in the daylight hours?)
We free singers be, baby,
tall walkers, high steppers,
hip shakers, we free singers be
still waters sometimes too.
(Remember, oh, do you remember
the days when children held our hands
and danced
around us in circles, and we laughed
in the sun, remember
how we slept in the shade of the trees
and woke, trembling in the darkness?)
We free singers be
voyagers
and sing of cities
with straight streets
and mountains piercing the moon—
and rivers that never run dry.
(Remember, oh, do you remember
the snow
falling

on broadway
and the soldiers marching
thru the icy streets
with blood on their coat sleeves.
remember how we left the warm movie house
turned up our collars
and rode the subway home?)
We free singers be, baby,
We free singers be.

Norbert Krapf

Village in Snowstorm

after a painting by Lucas
van. Valckenborch, 1586

Gnarled black limbs poke
into the eye of the storm.
A basket of provisions under
every motherly arm, a bundle
of tied twigs on every fatherly
shoulder, the villagers plod
through white falling upon white.
Children christen one another
with snowballs, skate in escape
across the village square.
Leather-shuttered horses, necks
arched against evening, drag
sleighs toward cottages. Soon
every hearth will flick flaming
tongues toward shadowy corners,
wine-warmed eyes will browse
through windows at the whiteness
filling up the night like a well.

John Knoepfle

At The Roadside

when someone fell
the others came
they picked up the broken glasses
the wristwatch with its shattered crystal
the hat in the dirt and the scarf
they recovered the lost shoe

they would stand there
looking at him for awhile
then go their way

they just said
well this is the end
this is the end of the world

Those Who Come What Will They Say Of Us

they were not good
our fathers
nothing went right for them

the signs of the times said
watch out and cut cha
and they worried about that

they could not take pity on themselves
they could not see
how all things
cried out to share them

Maxine Kumin

How It Goes On

Today I trade my last unwise
ewe lamb, the one who won't leave home,
for two cords of stove-length oak
and wait on the old enclosed
front porch to make the swap.
November sun revives the thick
trapped buzz of horseflies. The siren
for noon and forest fires blows
a sliding scale. The lamb of woe
looks in at me through glass
on the last day of her life.

Geranium scraps from the window box
trail from her mouth, burdock burrs
are stickered to her fleece like chicken pox,
under her tail stub, permanent smears.

I think of how it goes on,
this dark particular bent of our hungers:
the way wire eats into a tree
year after year on the pasture's perimeter
keeping the milk cows penned
until they grow too old to freshen;
of how the last wild horses were scoured
from canyons in Idaho, roped, thrown,
their nostrils twisted shut with wire
to keep them down, the mares aborting,
days later, all of them carted to town.

I think of how it will be
in January, nights so cold
the pond ice cracks like target practice,
daylight glue-colored, sleet falling,
my yellow horse slick with the ball-bearing
sleet, raising up from his dingy browse
out of boredom and habit
to strip bark from the fenced-in trees;

of February, month of the hard palate,
the split wood running out,
worms working in the flour bin.

The lamb, whose time has come, goes off
in the cab of the dump truck, tied to the seat
with baling twine, durable enough
to bear her to the knife and rafter.

O lambs! The whole wolf-world sits down to eat
and cleans its muzzle after.

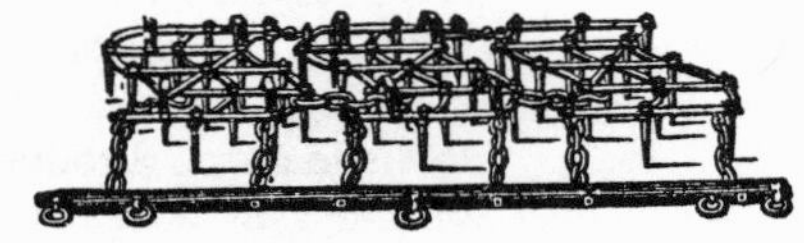

Randy Lane

Song

Sometimes in the fast food kitchen
in the mid-afternoon when business is slow
Betty the tiny amazing married Urbandale woman & I
sing together.

Today we sang "On Top of Old Smokey."

& we did what we do,
Betty at the east sink making one of her stupendous carnival salads,
ramming lettuce & red cabbage & carrots & spinach into the noisy
machine,
me at the west in my potato wrapture
occasionally humming or pipping or snurgling.

Later,
Betty punches off & goes home often to dirty dishes waiting
but gladly even so
& I fall stupidly in love with the blond sisters Linda & Sue
either one or both
almost every working day.

Denise Levertov

Writing to Aaron

(From a series, Homage to Pavese)

. . . after three years—a 3-decker novel
in fifteen pages? Which beginning
to begin with? 'Since I saw you last,
the doctor has prescribed me artificial tears,
a renewable order . . . ' But that leaves out
the real ones. Shall I write about them?
What about comedy, laughter, good news?
'I live in a different house now,
but can give you news
of most of the same people . . . ' That ignores
the significance of the house, its tone of voice,
and the sentence by sentence
unfolding of lives into chapters.
'Your last letter told about sand-dunes in winter,
and having the sea to yourself.
Beautiful; I read it to the strangers
in whose midst I was at the time.
And that's the way we lost touch for so long,
my response was the reading aloud
instead of a letter,
and we both moved house—
a shifting of sand underfoot . . .'

Well, I could echo
the sound of facts, their weather—
thunderclaps, rain hitting stone, rattle of windows.
And spaces would represent sunlight,
when the wind gave over and everyone rested
between the storms.
Or chronological narrative? 'In the spring
of '73,' . . . 'That summer,'
'By then it was fall . . . '
                                        All or nothing—
and that would be nothing,
dust, parchment dried up, invisible ink.
Maybe I'll leave the whole story

for you to imagine,
telling you only, 'A year ago,
I said farewell to that poplar you will remember,
that gave us its open secret,
pressed on us all we could grasp, and more,
of vibrating, silvergreen being,
a tree tripping over its phrases in haste,
eloquent aspen.'

I know you know
it took my farewell for granted:
what it had given, it would never take back.
I know you know
about partings, tears, eyedrops, revisions, dwellings, discoveries,
mine or yours; those are the glosses,
Talmudic tractates, a lifetime's study. The Word itself
is what we heard, and shall always hear, each leaf
imprinted, syllables in our lives.

Psalm—People Power at the Die-in

(The anti-nuclear die-in,
Washington, D.C., and the
official shutdown of the
Seabrook Plant, June 1978)

Over our scattered tents by night
lightning and thunder called to us.

Fierce rain blessed us,
catholic, all-encompassing.

We walked through blazing morning
into the city of law,

of corrupt order, of invested power.

By day and by night
we sat in the dust,

on the cement pavement we sat down and sang.

In the noon of a long day, sharing the work of the play,
we died together, enacting

the death by which all
shall perish unless we act.

* * *

Solitaries drew close, releasing
each solitude into its blossoming.

We gave to each other the roses
of our communion —

A culture of gardens, horticulture not agribusiness,
arbors among the lettuce, small terrains.

* * *

When we tasted the small, ephemeral
harvest of our striving,

great power flowed from us,
luminous, a promise. Yes! . . .

great energy flowed from solitude,
and great power from communion.

Philip Levine

My Son and I

In a coffee house at 3 am
and he believes
I'm dying. Outside the wind
moves along the streets
of New York City picking up
abandoned scraps of newspapers
and tiny messages of hope
no one hears. He's dressed
in worn corduroy pants

and shirts over shirts,
and his hands are stained
as mine once were
with glue, ink, paint.
A brown stocking cap
hides the thick blond hair
so unlike mine. For forty
minutes he's tried not
to cry. How are his brothers?
I tell him I don't know,
they have grown away
from me. We are Americans
and never touch on this
stunned earth where a boy
sees his life fly past
through a car window. His mother?
She is deaf and works
in the earth for days, hearing
the dirt pray and guiding
the worm to its feasts. Why
do I have to die? Why
do I have to sit before him
no longer his father, only
a man? Because the given
must be taken, because
we hunger before we eat,
because each small spark
must turn to darkness.
As we said when we were kids
and knew the names of everything
. . . just because. I reach
across the table and take
his left hand in mine.
I have no blessing. I can
tell him how I found
the plum blossom before
I was thirty, how once
in a rooming house in Alicante
a man younger than I,
an Argentine I barely understood,
sat by me through the night
while my boy Teddy cried out
for help, and how when he slept
at last, my friend wept

with thanks in the cold light.
I can tell him that his hand
sweating in mine can raise
the Lord God of Stones,
bring down the Republic of Lies,
and hold a spoon. Instead
I say it's late, and he pays
and leads me back
through the empty streets
to the Earle Hotel, where
the room sours with the mould
of old Bibles dumped down
the air-shaft. In my coat
I stand alone in the dark
waiting for something,
a flash of light, a song,
a remembered sweetness
from all the lives I've lost.
Next door the TV babbles
on and on, and I give up
and sway toward the bed
in a last chant before dawn.

Spring in the Old World

In the central terminal rain pouring
through the broken glass on the trains below,
loading and unloading. Above the gray dome
the great sky twisting in from the North Sea.
Cold, wet, wondering, I stood in a corner.
A dark boy walked in off the streets, a shepherd
born of shepherds. At 14 come to Tetuan
for work, then to Ceuta, Algeciras, Amsterdam.
His robes black now with rain, he cracks
sunflower seeds between his teeth, *pipas*
he calls them, and spits the shells and laughs.
In the lower Atlas the hills are green
where his brothers and he raced
through the long grass and wildflowers,
shouting to the air, their skirts
flared out around them, open and burning.

Larry Levis

Weldon Kees

10 p.m., the river thinking
Of its last effects,
The bridges empty. I think
You would have left the party late,

Declining a ride home.
And no one notices, now,
The moist hat brims
Between the thumbs of farmers

In Beatrice, Nebraska.
The men in their suits
Bought on sale, ill fitting,
The orange moon of foreclosures.

And abandoning the car!
How you soloed, finally,
Lending it the fabulous touch
Of your absence.

You'd call that style—
To stand with an unlit cigarette
In one corner of your mouth,
Admiring the sun on Alcatraz.

Crystal MacLean

The Good Woman

The girl he married
because she was a good woman—
the salad girl in the cafeteria at Michigan State
the wholesome one
with the second best figure at the pool
who wanted just to be held sometimes
who gave him a son too soon, typed his thesis,
and screamed a lot
the one who read a lot, was so understanding,
could talk to animals so well
the one who went for help
to stop screaming
and learned that books are her friends
who finally learned she did not need
to be wholesome, who could write her
own thesis, the one who left
and stopped screaming

Thomas McGrath

Travelling Song

I was a laughing child
I was born in a happy year
But the wind that blew from afar
Sang hunger in my ear.
It shaped my eye to a tear.

I was born with an easy mind
To stay where I was born;
But the wind that blew from afar,

It sang of a great wrong;
It's how my heart was torn.

Now I am put upon
To travel and lament.
Though born to a happy place
The wind would not consent.
How strange now is my face,
And how my life is rent.

John Carey's Second Song

I

The Hotel Peine Forte et Dure in Santa Monica
................................and go in there:
Being too tired to drive home,
Or no home to drive to anyway.

II

And go in there to the echoing fatigue in the thin sheets;
To wallpaper held up by a kind of intramural
Desperation . . . out of the dark
Streets with their little flares of sex and drugs,
With the panhandlers and the drunks in the doorways,
At the end of the line, one jump away from salt water,
Beyond the riches of neon and the country of houses.

III

And go in there.
This would be the end of the night except
This night has no end love has
No name this coffin has no handles
This room is, in its rationality,
A sort of end.

IV

But the end of the night? Now four hours
Until morning, the high workaday sun
Of unending midnight.
And go in there. And sleep.

Joe-Anne McLaughlin

Another Mother and Child

It must be spring, the way the light
almost misses the water, both of you
in bonnets, looking in different directions.
Her coat is a dark velvet, my mother's coat
was also velvet, but bright red,
and it was spring, but night, no lazy lake
in the distance, but an avenue, my mother
a delicate she-bear, with me in hand, charging
up it, after father who must have seen us
coming, because we missed him by minutes.
My mother screaming: You men. You Irish.
Good Friday—for shame, go home to your families.
Presenting me to the men as if I were some
cruel miracle, her stigmata. The men laughing
their heads off and not even knowing my mother
was Jewish. My face, the picture of my father's,
as red as my mother's coat, the faces
of those drinking men. How I hated them
for scorning my mother, her for scorning my father.
Still, we'd have our Easter bonnets,
and walking to the Art Museum that spring,
people would smile at us, and sometimes we'd smile
too, so that not even an artist, a Renoir,
could have told the difference.

Sally McNall

Metaphors

Perhaps
they are trying to tell us
something
the botched babies
the one with flippers
the one with
                    the long split tongue
the one
          with his heart outside
                                        his rib cage
About ocean
about
          language
about a world so gentle—

Gerard Malanga

What I Have Done

I remove a red cement slab in the dead of night
and carve a monument to myself: a
basrelief-standing figure in profile and
mountains just beginning to rise and my name
chiseled in Roman type off to the right.

I return to the scene of the crime
and the dirt patch in front of the
house is roped off. The owner paces
back and forth. A feeling of sadness
surrounds this house.

I want to re-set the slab in its
proper place but cannot scrape
off my name.

J. J. Maloney

Poems from Prison

Day after day after day
he trudges to work
with a mouthful of cobwebs.

He sits and mutters
about working conditions—
the arrogant Lieutenant
the dull-headed Warden
the stingy tax-payers
But he does not quit.

Is he Menninger's *Man Against Himself?*—
who volunteers for prison
8 hours a day . . .
paying for hub-caps stolen
20 years ago . . .
An unresolved oedipal complex
etcetera.
Does he know where he needs to be
And put himself there
Eight hours a day?

2. They have built us a golf course
where we putt and putter—
chuckle and laugh.
They have built it in a shady place,
in the shadow of a 22 foot
wall and when our low
frustration threshold is reached
we rap out a 400 yard drive as catharsis . . .
One second later the wall opens its grey mouth
and spits the yellow-checkered ball back
on the green saving us
the dollar-ten price of therapy.
When we finish our game
they smile
And march us back to our cells.

Someone, I think, noticed that they hang
Tires
In the Drill cage at the zoo.

Freya Manfred

Grandma Shorba and The Pure In Heart

My mother's mother's underpants
made me not want to grow up.
And my belief that she kept an ax
in the top of her old-fashioned chain toilet
convinced me I wouldn't live that long anyway.
                    She used to sneak into the bathroom
at midnight for the ax,
and search to kill me,
because she knew I suspected
she was secretly a murderer.
                    She saw me notice
the thin warts, like rice grains,
growing on end out of her neck.
She saw me stare at her long floppy breasts
and the pink, wide-legged underpants
falling off her hips.
The crotch hung down like a handle,
not wide enough to hide
mouse nest pubic hair,
less grey than her head hair.
                    I was so glad I had skinny underpants
and an eel's rear end,
glad I did not have to stir tired bones
to make tea for visitors all day,
or feed the men who begged quarters, bread, and wine
at the pantry door.
                    I figured she used that ax at night
after giving in all day
to people who took advantage.
                    She was so NICE.
She had to have something else going for her.

Grandmothers
have caused me a lot of trouble and pity.
                    Like my great-grandmother in Iowa.
She died. But somehow when we drove back to Minnesota
after the funeral, she was lying in the oblong space
between the front and back seat of my dad's Ford.

In the front seat Dad and Uncle Floyd teased each other
about the correct grip for newfangled steering wheels,
their faces alight in the glow of speedometer, clock,
and gas gauges.
                    I was curled into a ball
in the dark caverns of the back seat.
Smack between me and the joke-cracking men lay my
dead great-grandmother, who wanted to snatch me,
because I ate four ham sandwiches and the whole plate
of mints at her funeral, despite the heavy smell of rotten
gums and perfumed moth balls.
                    Lucky Dad was around, because she glared,
fierce and very positive about something,
her eyes like live coals on the floor of the car,
                    so completely dead when I wasn't.

My worst "grandmother" was May Belle Harmer,
my day care nurse, a "lovely woman," who loved me
"very much," mother said.
But May Belle would not let me straddle the toilet
and pee facing the wall like Dad.
"Teeny gals harn't made that way."
                    I wanted to be like Dad,
glancing amiably out the window at the pine trees,
staring at the fly specks on the wall,
casual and leisurely,
                    NOT facing front,
committed to a seat, staring at May Belle's slitty eyes,
pursed lips, stomach like a cow (and gurgling like a cow too).
"Face front!" she'd shout.
Under my breath she was Old Mad Hatter and March Hare.
                    As soon as she left,
I swiveled and faced the wall.
Then I could relax, lean my elbows on the flat top
of the toilet tank, like at a Woolworth's lunch counter,
and pour myself lemon sodas from Mother's powder box.

May Belle didn't trust Woolworth's lunch counters
because of the germs drunk people left on the salt and pepper.
When she saw a drunk man in the street,
she shriveled up her jowls and ushered me away.
                    I preferred going out

with my mother's mother, Grandma Shorba
(of the underpants) and talking with the drunk men.
No sooner did we spot a White Castle than we'd be
at the counter for a treat. I could order six Castleburgers
without a struggle from Grandma Shorba, and eat them
on the bus home.
                    And at home she had Easter Eggs,
cream-filled chocolates, caraway soup with dumplings
and poppyseed rolls. My favorite dessert was licorice nibs
and cucumbers with cream. During dinner I sang,
                    "Dog, dog, sing a happy sog."
Grandma shouted, "So*n*g, so*n*g, you silly goose, not *sog*.
There's no such word."
                    Both giggling, because the business
of fitting rhyme to meaning could go too far,
and make you sober as a judge.

After dinner Grandma Shorba went to church
to hear Missionary Fern and her husband, Billy Jean.
                    If her legs ached, she stayed home
and read the obituaries, of people she knew and people
she didn't know, to me.
                    She finished with accounts of auto accidents.
She read about mangled blond girls with severed heads,
broken hearts, and tortured legs, in some drunken
highway pile-up.
                    "Lord have mercy,"
twitching the paper and her cheeks, hitching up her eyeglasses.
                    She showed me a photograph
of her only son, George,
who died in a motorcycle-car accident when he was fifteen.
                    George had one arm draped over the silver-
studded saddle, one leg cocked on the cycle runner. Grandma
had hung a red-padded cloth heart over the corner of the
photograph, which I still see
                    as clearly as the thumbprints I left,
on the carefully shined glass.
                    "George was young and proud and beautiful,"
Grandma said. "He begged me for a birthday motorcycle. God
forgive me, I bought it for him." She showed me where she had
written in a diary:
                    It is God's will
                    that he did not want George to suffer here.

He was too sweet and good,
and called home long before his allotted time.
Since that time I have not lived,
waiting for that meeting day in my Father's
house, as He has promised.
On the bottom of the page she added:
The Pure In Heart shall see God.
No one in this life could take Georgie's place.

A few years before George was born, Grandma herself was startled
and run over by a speeding car. She said she broke all the bones
in her body except two. She pulled her skirt up to show me a
purple crescent-shaped gouge on the inside of her knee.
I stared at the puckered skin grafts
and told her it looked like a horse had stomped her with one hoof.
She said it felt like 100 hooves.
After hearing the obituaries
and chanting "Jesus Loves Me" with Grandma,
I crawled into bed and lay awake
with my back against Grandma's warm back. She snored,
vibrating steadily against me. I rubbed the delicate skin
of my wrists back and forth over the hairy sheets Grandma
bought in basement sales.
I pictured Grandma being run over, stomped,
and the shiver of her bones, and the slivers.
I summoned the flash of her hidden ax in the toilet top,
sharp for her next
retaliatory midnight outing.

It was amazing how Grandma forgot where she put everything,
so when we went to the movies we were always late.
"It's just that I've had so much trouble,"
she said, "in life."
That's why her glasses were in the silverware tray
and why her gloves were not beside her hat.
Dear Jesus usually helped her find them,
though I kept a sharp eye out myself.
Sometimes I got so mad looking for Grandma's hat pin,
that I pinched her arms and the rolls of fat at her waist
all the way to the movies, shrieking like a harpy,
leaping away from the slaps of her fingers.
"Stop that!" she said.

"Now keep still. Keep still."
"I won't. I'll talk all during this dumb movie."
"You keep still."
"You owe me two dollars for candy, Grandma," I concluded.
"Hussst! You keep still,
and I'll tell you a good parrot story:
In a cold attic in the Old Country two blue-lipped
servant girls worked for a bare living.
Their rich mistress wore a gorgeous green wool dress
and a gold locket. She owned a fat green parrot
who croaked, 'Polly wants! Polly wants!' at the
servant girls, while they stayed up all night
sewing fancy new dresses for the lady.
The girls got mad"
(Grandma's lips twitched and she got a gleam in her eye.)
"so one night
they stitched up the parrot's hind end with a green
thread. The lady kept feeding her parrot until it died."
I squirmed for the world's dumb animals when Grandma concluded:
"The parrot couldn't tell the lady its problem."

We still weren't at the movies, because Grandma
walked slow with her badly-mended legs.
I kept dancing ahead into the darkest shadows,
so she told me another story
about a man, crippled worse than she was after her car accident,
who got trapped in midstreet by an oncoming trolly.
He lay down to pray
between two trolly tracks, and got up untouched when the car
passed over him. (Dear Jesus again.)

Grandma said Jesus could see around corners,
so I kept him for my friend when I went out alone
in the woods or the high swamp grass.
Grandma said
Jesus loved little girls like me,
but he shouldn't take me away like he took George.
"Why did he take George, Grandma?"
"Because he was always too good for this world,
my own precious boy,
God forgive me."

God forgive you?
Dear Grandma, please, before I get old
or run over by a car, I forgive you.
Do you forgive me?
                    I forgive everything,
even the image of your underpants,
that makes me quake with laughter this morning
and reach down to touch my unprotected self.
                    I'm going to sew
a padded red heart
for my own true dead love's photograph,
and make care-away soup
for my own boy or girl.
And I don't expect you
to come back from the grave
into my house or my car at midnight
                    with an ax or anything.
I understand
you're much happier there with Jesus.

Jesus would still be with me too,
but I found a horse named Chita Maria.
                    If it hadn't been for you
                    I wouldn't have owned that horse.
You couldn't stand to hear me cry
young honey tears all night,
so you gave Dad money for Chita Maria
and a silver-studded saddle.
                    It's a good thing, Grandma.
That horse was the first dancing friend
I loved so much I could have died.
I grew up
so I could ride her alone
across the Minnesota River.

                    I hope you are doing well
                    with George and the flying ghosts
                    in your Father's house
                    where you belong,
                    you sweet, you startled woman,
                    you burdened heart
                    of my heart.

Marya Mannes

The First

How can a long-used body reconstrue
the time of innocence? The mind must strain
backward across old knowledge to the new,
unstroked, unpenetrated flesh; the pain
of nipples hardening to the boyish touch,
the pulse of sudden heat . . . and yes, the round
smooth neck of youth, the sudden alarm of such
hard arms, hard lips, the insistent tongue, the sound
of breathing. But then, they were each somehow afraid,
so young they were, so troubled in ignorance
they did not dare go further. And so they stayed
kissing and clinging in a murmurous trance,
over and over whispering other's name—
until, one day, he hurt her as he came.

Age

Desire flickers like candles in the wind
and like them wavers and then gutters out.
The important head on which the hair has thinned,
the body in which the years have put to rout
the power to rise—these stretch beside the claim
of their affection. Nothing is said, but hand
holds neighboring hand as woman remembers when
this man was conqueror and could command
body and soul beyond all other men.
Now, office, domesticity, and strain
have emasculated him, who can still impale
on lesser minds the acute spear of his brain
but, anguished, cannot call himself a male.
And yet he is, if woman holds him dear
and lets her arms sustain him in their sphere.

E. L. Mayo

On the Night Train from Oxford

Once we were small and real
Who in this freezing shell
Whisk through the dark. The guard
Who slammed the door of our cell

Shut sight from our eyes;
So swiftly turn the wheels
We cannot feel what we know,
We cannot know what we feel.

A number of years ago
Hulme took the classic view:
Man is limited,
He said, but the world said *No.*

Man is boundless and good
And will make all things new
Look out the window, Look
At what we have done and do.

By this compartment flit
The fragments of an age.
Who can put back together
Our bombed-out heritage?

Today at New College
Epstein's *Lazarus*
Heard one call his name,
Rose, towered over us,

Loomed in his cerement,
Twisting his narrow head
Back and *Up* to the Word
Compelling him from the dead.

Surely Epstein knew
It could speak to anyone,
Gentile or Jew, even
To one on this night train.

Envoi

Running out of town on a rail is too good for
The little king and his sister
They say who yesterday
(The good days seem so far!)
We threw up our hats, shouted ourselves hoarse for.

"Wisdom will die with you . . . vox populi"
The preacher says, and no doubt it's true, though
If this wheel keeps turning over and over,
Who'll put a spoke in it or brake the day
When they are suddenly we, we suddenly they?

Goodbye then, little princess and little king,
For awhile. We cannot honestly entertain
Hope for you now, but neither can we deny
That somewhere an ear already hears the barrow
Rumbling on stone that will run us out tomorrow.

The Doomed City

The doomed city we live in
Is crumbling while we sit
Discussing it.

The clock upon the height
Moves interminably from left to right
But we are not
Interminable. "I'm

Very gloomy about things
But you have to make yourself
Keep trying anyway,"
Said Bobby Kennedy

Knowing eternity
Does not open to the bodily eye.
We must look far
Inward to perceive
Here in the doomed city where we live
The city that will not die.

Stone

Look at a stone and it's nothing,
Something to kick against, but look at the
Same stone twenty years later
And you feel yourself vanishing in perspective into thin air.

There have always been sacred stones
And this must be one reason: stone's soul
Came to its confirmation, conformation
So ploddingly

It clings to one idea
While we go on to others smaller, smoother
Than the granite boulder
That struck the armed guard from the tomb door
And set the prisoner free,

Stupor mundi, amazement of beholders.
Thank you, stone
For being of the same opinion still
For being Peter, whom
We shall deny, return to, differ from
Until the sky is rolled up like a scroll
And all the stars fall down.

A Fair Warning

Practically everyone goes to the Petrified Forest
As visitor or tourist,
Staying no longer than permits of the barest
"We drove through Saturday. Every contortion
Of those grim trunks staggers imagination."

But once in a great while among these strong
Motionless boughs and leaves unwhispering
One stands as if he heard
A petrified bird
And stays long.

The Stones of Sleep

The Germans rub it on
The walls of their houses.
The gray, transparent stone
Assures the inhabitant
No matter what he does, what he has done
A sleep so plaisant and so wholesome
As he may never wholly waken from.

To the Young Rebels

What the heart wants comes true.
Therefore be sure you
Do what you want. Look how many
Condescend to war's felicity. Stare

Where you will, you will discover no
Alternative hid from the trilobite;
History is adamant: you
Are what *it* willed to do.

Oh wonderful consensus! *Schrechlichkeit*
Falls from the air. Certainly
Men of low degree are vanity
And men of high a lie. So now
When all men know
That Gabriel has a horn
Able to blow
Rebellion and the Establishment alike
To the ionosphere, now, if you know
What you want, do, do, do, do, do.

Failure

Failure is more important than success
Because it brings intelligence to light
The bony structure of the universe.

At The Louvre

After so many larger canvases
I thought with surprise at first *How small she is*
Next I grew aware she was looking at me
Smiling a little like a good hostess
To put me at my ease, but also
To know me through and through. Leonardo
Had her eyes; they are hers now
To study all who pass until the lens
Blur or the world run out of specimens.

Note on Modern Journalism During the Last Campaign

Butter and ink
Butter and ink
When we have enough butter
We print what we think,

But ink without butter
Ink without butter
And we publish whatever
You want us to utter.

Of Angels

Your angel weighs heavier than your mortal.
It hurts like hell if you run into one.
Only one wrestler ever made an angel cry uncle.

When they leap off the world it is as though
Washington Monument flew,
The whole world wobbles like a soap-bubble. Hang on!
One will be leaving any minute now.

Mbembe Milton Smith

Did They Help Me At The State Hospital For The Criminally Insane?

For this one
You need a pocket dictionary
That enters biblical charity
As a synonym for atrocities
Committed in a silent
Partner's best interest.
Cleave end & mean,
Wall them, pin them
In antagonistic corners,
Departmentalize, dissect them
'Til the sense in such nonsense
Is twisted loose. Say "normal"
By all means, by any means
Is correct, justified.
Don't question this!
Declare a holy war on madness,
But stay unmoved by it all like god,
Keep the goal aloft.
& if the goal is missed,
A fraction too long
On the electroshock machine,
A little too much Haldol,
Be quick & resolute with disclaimer.

Then i suppose things could be compared.
Did Truman help the Japs?
By saving countless Kamikazes
From thoughtless death?
Did Hitler help the Jews?
With Jewish enterprise?
Sticktogetherness?
At least the bathwater

Finds its way home to sea.
So when the baby
Who was thrown out with it
Grows up despite all odds
Having drunk his fill
Of castor-oil reality
& held it on his stomach,
Commend the state's parental guidance,
Shake its rank statutory hand.
The state has made a man.

Yeah, they helped me.

John Bowles

Robert Mezey

The Celebration

1

What if this man with his rough head
His two hands without jewels
Pretended he was a king
He is a king
Who else would be sitting beside you

2

If you had not come
I would have been
With this woman that woman
I would have danced
With an immense wall
My forehead frozen to the stone
To no music
I would have been

3

I took you in the abandoned church
With sweat pouring down
The guests departed
The ghosts gathered around us
Under the mountain
We celebrated with our love wine
The lock blown off the door
The door leaning

4

You lean back into the night of the almonds
In the seventh year a blossom

Vassar Miller

Eden Revisited

"We'll talk all night until we swoon away," you promised,
friend of my innocence and of no more than that,
the only rule allowing us to talk.

*

Words were my lawyers once before Judge Life.
Now when he passes sentence,
silence and I stand side by side.

No longer are words the currency in my country.
I have been thrown into jail
more times than one for passing counterfeit.

*

My mother's best friend gave a leaf to her.
She recorded it in words, saying,
"Given to me in 1912 by Helen."

Though Freud was lurking those days in Vienna,
bidding us unravel our lives in words,
people still spoke.

And those two girls, my mother and Helen,
not knowing Victoria was dead,
still moved inside their skins as though not touching them.

So, now I view their leaf, more durable than breath,
but bruised and breaking under each minute more,
frayed reconciliation between truth and lie.

A Clash With Cliches

The peace in the valley will sing to me like a choir
when the end of a perfect day laughs at me wryly.
I shall lie in the grass of green pastures as in the
  trough of a wave
that has washed me clean of the day
as I lean back to finger the scars of a good fight
like a lonesome child who plays with himself.
Oh, it will be good to get out of the wind
after a high on the raindrops,
for sleep is smoother than wine, swifter than prayer,
  sweeter than love
in that time when all the clichés standing tiptoe
take flesh of my tired bones.

Awkward Goodbyes

I am sorry I seldom speak I
am losing my knack I
remember the language but poorly.

Though God knows I used it well, spoke it
better than you even I
take small pride in such talent I

sucked it up more easily than mother's
milk. It must taste sweeter
to odd palates. Anyhow I'm

craving amnesia, the happy kind,
since whatever pig-
latin we talked, none called it love.

Ralph J. Mills, Jr.

Chelsea Churchyard

Crowded gravestones,
brothers, sisters in silence,
lean together and touch.

Walling the church's stained bulk
as it weathers another century,
they're ignorant how wind and rain
have whitened their thin shoulders
like a January snow.

Given away, names, stones,
grain after grain,
they need no one, nothing
but to be
where their shadows meet.

Grasses

(after Harry Callahan)

Scattered among stiff black stalks,
whips, scrolls of light:
fine traceries
drawn over a dark field.

Grasses twine together,
or bow apart
in arches to tunnels of shadow.

A dry ocean is rustling its song
across the night ground,
moonless
and without paths.

Only the delicate blades
point away:
bent by the wind
their edges shine.

Virginia Scott Miner

Nichols Fountain

(Kansas City)

Rome has its fountains. This
is not from that older world,
beautiful, weary. This
is a fountain that speaks
of horrors within, without.
Terrified horses strain,
besieged by incredible monsters
while oblivious cherubs play
with cattails and fishes.

Sitting one day by the fountain,
watching its waters rise
in a sparkling central plume
before, from basin to basin,
they fell to the lower pool,
I asked a young boy beside me
"Why do you like this fountain?"
"Because," he said at once,
"no matter how I feel,
it says something to me—always."

And twice I saw a young man
facing that turmoil, that power,
and blowing a child's toy horn—
one tone, insistent, strong.

Mad—he was certainly mad—
yet a Roland at Roncesvaux.

Stay away from this fountain
if you must have something pretty.

Frederick Morgan

Bones

The bones go under the soil, under the soil
at year's end the bones go under the soil—
sometimes they wave red flags
sometimes they speak not at all

The bones are boats that go sailing in the black ground
clean through the earth and out the other side
in an every-day kind of way
into the sun again

The bones speak to the birds, the birds sing back
but the language is lost before it comes to the ears
of fools who run to and fro
between the birds and the bones

I killed a fool once and drank blood from his skull
and taking his bony fingers in my hand
asked him where he wanted to go:
he didn't say yes, he didn't say no

Bones have a home underground or so I'm told.
They are themselves the city in which they dwell
and have a meaning, too, since they once were we:
another meaning is coming, wait and see

Edward Morin

Notes on the Post-Industrial Revolution

I didn't mind the bosses' pistol-whipping
six shy Mexicans: their bruises hardly showed.

Chains fit those Chinamen well: who saw them
once the slave boat pulled away from shore?

I never wanted power enough to change things:
computers work everything out, including me.

Some newspapers say we're robbing the poor,
but we're only doing the best we can.

Sunny days! oh sunny, sunny, sunny, days:
there ain't nothing in the world, you know,

like lying in your blood with your radio.
Even a good wind blows some ill.

Hilda Morley

The Nike of Samothrace

For Stefan, who loved her

There she is
                    (John said
coming round the corner
of the hall
                & we turned to the stairway
                to find her standing
in that wind that charged her
                                        in
a forward movement
                        (yours in
                        your life
                                & to
                        the very end in
                        the speaking
                        of your eyes)
lit up by the air where there is
no quietude,
                    no final
compromise
                    (no falseness
                    of acceptance
or by water   broken
into light continually,

because the reach is farther
always & ahead,   though
firm in the wind,
                    & aware of
danger—
            That wing that rises
above her in the fullness
of her courage
              knows nothing
that cannot be transformed,
                              knows of
no water unstirring

John W. Moser

Sea Food Thought

She sidled up to me coyly and said,
"Boop, boop, dit-a-da-dum whatum chew?"

I was nonplused by this but immediately
regained my senses and replied
"Food-a-la-rack-a-sacky want some seafood
mama."

We then placed our webbing hands around
each other and walked off into the sunset
towards the silent sea.

Room Service

I've been sitting around for weeks reading
Kierkegaard, Nietzche, Camus, Sartre.

Today I pick up the Kansas City Star. In
the Art Section, Jess Ritter quotes Fats
Domino, "If I've got a telephone, a television,
my Bible, and room service, what more do I need."

Howard Moss

A Colloquy with Gregory on the Balcony

Now tell me again about Miss Teller's dog.
You were up on the balcony? Yes? And then?
You felt an irresistible desire to smash . . .
Oh, *push*. I'm sorry. I see. And when
The moon shone down on her leg like satin
So even the finest porous nylon
Thickened with longing . . . Something snapped?
A synapse, perhaps? The mind has traps . . .
I'm *not* attacking you. I see what you mean:
The moon changes things. I've been affected myself.
I *am* affected? I didn't come here to be . . .
If you feel that way, why I think I'll be . . .
No, no, forget that. This is all so ghastly!
Of *course*, I support you. Now take it ea . . .
Naturally I respect your desire to be
*Some*body. I'm with you all the way,
In spite of the sordid . . . Yes. I mean
If you try real hard you can often see
Why people are crazy . . . Gregory, plea-
se, get back inside! I was pulling your leg!
Be reasonable! Stop! For God's sake! *Greg*! . . .

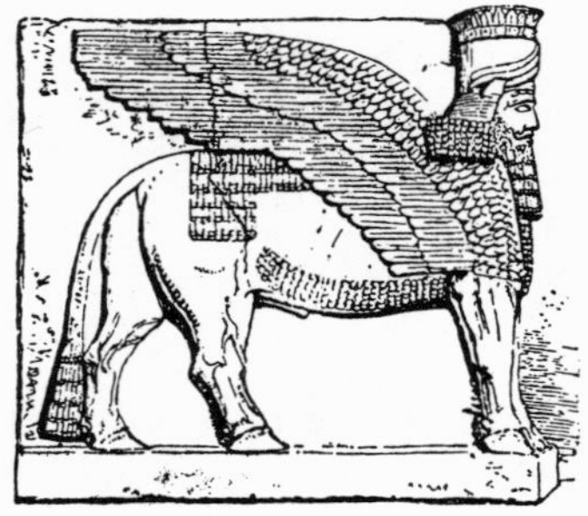

G. E. Murray

Shelby County, Ohio. November 1974

In our smoke house,
in hot fog of hickory and buckeye chips,
we hang meats

like vignettes, independent
of all but the bones
we crack

and soup. Outside,
it's the same white, shimmering
Ohio country

we trust like an open palm,
like an apothecary.
And it's this same crosswind

feeding fire
that begins stirring in us like dusk,
that cures like smoke.

Art Sinsabaugh

Tom O'Grady

Aubade After The Party

The sun finds your eye
We have made it through the night
Food burns in the kitchen as our heads
Fall together.
I can feel your breath this morning
Coming apart like ash.

Downstairs, the strawberries are sliced
In the light, the cereal stares,
Our toast is matched for us.
Someone who could not make it home
Swirls the orange juice
The cats clang cymbals in the trash
The milk smells like sleep.

But you say this food is day music,
Tempting us out of dreaming,
Dancing before last night's dishes
Like a thief.

Roger Pfingston

Dave Oliphant

A Little Something For William Whipple

Back & forth on the criss-crossing walks,
building to brick building of then Lamar Tech,
changing of classes in a blinding white light,
though no St. Paul, just a coastal sun in summer.
Choking through smog & fumes, drifting in
from adjacent refinery or the sulphur pits,
sitting beneath a crop of loblolly, stunted pine,
unreaching to rooftops of gravel & tar—
all to me a veritable Garden,
at the very least a Texas Eden.

Where library assignments you made,
even now with a Ph.D.
I still wouldn't pass such tests,
climb to heights your search required:
newspapers from Boston in '73,
an obscure note on Poe, in French,
couldn't find them to save my soul.
Boiled in your scholarly hell,
shoulder to the research stone,
only to have it roll back down.

Then in from humid heat to freeze between
refrigerated stacks & colder stares,
from a lady librarian at the reference desk,
trying again to discover at last
the why of Samuel Johnson's long fear of death,
while a yellow fog engulfed the campus, filled
the halls, was Heaven to me,
and just to breathe the novels
you taught in a huff
worth finishing with a stigma C.

A Mexican Scrapbook

Along the highway street,
a block before the plaza,
with its blue-tiled benches
of mountain & maguey scenes
he knew deeper than the picturesque,

his dark-clad wave of mourners rolls,
its crest a blue-gray metal gleam
riding to church on shoulders like his
accustomed to the carrying
of over-sized sacks, clover

cut at dawn — heavy with wet,
goats, turkeys, kindling,
scented limbs of eucalyptus,
his own lifted here above the flow
of a tourist traffic slowed by

death's invisible dam,
as the memories now flood back
of their friend once gladly bore
burdens like this to market & mass,
afterwards to drink pulque or beer

in bars with louvered doors,
supported home by adobe walls,
a compadre's arms, the tiles & trees
of Atlixco, no sight we'd pay to see,
unmarked on any map or guide.

Elder Olson

Merry Christmas!

Santa Claus lies dead across the chair,
Shrunk to his elements—cap, suit, boots, and beard—
His swollen imposture ended, again exposed
As merely one more customary lie
Of all our numberless customary lies;
A myth I lent my substance; in itself
A dead thing that had never been alive;

Fitting saint of a false universe
Of false trees glittering with false fruits, false snow,
Of cozy uninhabitable pasteboard towns,
Paper bells, tin angels, plastic elves
—Tinselled pretence, mostly tomorrow's trash.
What? —Tell us cold is warm and dark is bright
When all about us, in the freezing night—?

Pack him away. We make myths, they make us;
Mere images of human hopes and fears,
Having only such power upon us as we give them,
Yet having such power, such power—pack him away,
Saint Liar, Saint Hypocrite. Did I "make the children happy?"
Must we deceive, then, to bring happiness?
—Then happiness itself is a deceit.

How is it that creatures craving truth
Contrive these lies, live these lies, at last
Are lived by these lies? Must such lies be told
Because the truth is more than we can bear?
O all our history, all our history!
O intolerable last error of Oedipus:
Better be blind than see what we must see.

Anthony Ostroff

Love

The people watch the young
lovers. They have told them what
to do and what not to do.
They are ravenous in their watching.
They are hoping for a mistake.
The boy touches the girl.
She cries out. Her hair is as long
as the wind. It entangles him.
Gently he tries to ease free.
He has no wish to hurt
the girl. Only to tell
tales of her hair, her hair
that is like a ladder let down
from a place, from a place. He will name
the place. He calls it "Heaven."
She smiles. She turns her face
to the boy. She sees he is strong.
"I am strong," she says. "Touch
me as you like." He leaps
into her hair. He begins to tear
it out by the roots. "Ah!"
she cries in ecstasy,
and wraps her hair round his neck
in a noose. In joy he pulls
and pulls until she is bald.
Her bare skull is bleeding.
Her eyes by whose light and her lips
by whose song the boy would have climbed
forever are withered and dim
now that her hair is gone.
She cannot forgive
the boy whose eyes bulge and lips
explode as he hangs from heaven.
The people nod and applaud.

War

The people love war.
"Let us have war!"
they cry. They cry
for war to each other.
They cry to their leader.
"Hear us!" they cry.
"We thirst for war.
We hunger for war.
We are sleepless for war,
to dream of war.
Oh let us have war!
What we need is war!
All is impure
except for war.
Consider! Consider!
It is better than peace,
it is better than water,
it is better than food,
it is better than wine.
It is better than love,
it is more than hate.
War! War!
It is better than prayer,
better than we are,
better than church,
better than art,
better than even
the art of war.
War is perfectible!
Let us have war!
Let us try again!"

End of the War in Merida

Furnace for a life that's done,
this wet, tropical place
dries in the sun of Cancer,
& the scorched cells of my soul,
wet from their red bath, dry
& swell with dryness, mad

to natural law, & run
from burning red coal to coal,
& swoon for joy in their own char
here in the courtyard garden of our
Colonial Hotel. O Beautiful,
so foreign, flowering, aflame!
We're here for this, & kiss
amid the garden's blaze.
Though Penance play with Pride
& all that grows decay
in the ripe, unholy sun,
we are innocent.
This holiday, personal,
exotic, paid, is our last one.

Robert Pack

The Ring

Easing the ring down her finger, he hears noon
    apple branches arc
above them; not one twig obscures their sight
    as they search beyond
each other for an instant, and return.
    With lines etched fine
as in an apple bud, on the gold band,
    a lady receives
her wedding ring in what must be
    reflected light,
for I think the circle above signifies
    the moon. Perhaps
the trees around them arc with the weight of fruit
    that glimmer in the pond
where poised ducks doubly glide in rows,
    or else wind loads
each apple with a weight more than its own.
    Though lord and lady hold
in place, he looks beyond her where the ring
    reveals a couple
entering a house. Over the doorway
    hovers an angel,
haloed, welcoming them in, though perhaps

only his mother
sees this form if he assumes the couple
are his parents
as they were. He cannot hear their words
that warm the room
as owl calls cross the shingles to the clouds.
Perhaps she asks him
if his mother, when her husband died,
gave her son this ring
on which his father weds his wife
who stares beyond him
for an instant, fixed in moonlight, and away
into the apple tree,
beside the pond, her daughter climbs. Perhaps
he sees her too,
reflected in her mother's eyes,
as I now see
my daughter whitely in procession
on her wedding day
with apple branches arced above her hair
that catches sunlight
like the moon. I hand the groom the ring
and step back in the house,
an angel guards, beside the moonlit window
where my mother paused,
when her husband died, and turned the ring half-circle
where the lord and lady
cannot see. And there, reversed, again
she waits in apple light,
as slow wind shifts the laden petals
in her hair, the pond,
under the tree, for him to wed her now,
as I do thee.

Philip Parisi

Niagara Falls

Far, far from the water's fall,
How the joy is drowned in cries of "No" and "No"—
Love becomes emergency—how it does not matter
That this is no place true lovers go.
How the rooms are full of those waiting to be laughed at.

Linda Pastan

Why Not?

Why not try again, although the past
in all its fine detail seems infinite?
I close my eyes and it's like putting on glasses.
The old landscapes jump into focus: grass
greener than grass; my surgeon father so anxious
to heal he drinks his coffee standing up;
my small bed angled into my small room
like a barge that might carry me into
my own dream of a future. Everything

I expected has long since happened.
Everything I wanted I took— but
always too early or too late.
Still there may be time. The old ladies
of Cambridge with bookbags and bicycles
laugh through faded teeth and beckon. To them
failure is just another rough cobblestone.
They say about loving, about riding
a bicycle: you never forget how.

Karl Patten

Wreathmakertraining

"Born in Berlin in 1926, and trained as a wreathmaker."
—biographical note in an anthology of German poets

I'm displaying here my authentic Yankee ignorance:
"trained as a wreathmaker"????

In our USA we train everybody for something believing
That we cannot tolerate waste and that all the moving parts

Of the good society must be an internal combustion engine.
But we do not train wreathmakers.

Deutschland is different and for me there will always be
Amazements emerging from those black forests and frozen plains.

Thus, wreathmakertraining. If you have training you have schools;
Ergo, there are wreathmakertraining schools in Germany.

Wreathmakertraining in Germany:

Erste Kurs: frosted Kris Kringles for Weihnachts, berries attached.
Zweite Kurs: bridal wreaths interlaced with white ribbons.
Dritte Kurs: honors for returning victors, Eisen Kreuz mit Swastika.
Vierte Kurs: black leaves on barbed wire with salt tears.
(The latter open only to those born circa 1926.)

We, in our USA, do not train wreathmakers.
Could it be that we neither celebrate nor mourn?

Robert Peterson

Robert's Rules of Order

"A group of 37 Scouts and 3 leaders left Thursday on a 22-day expedition that will include gold panning in New Mexico mountain streams. They are headed for the Scout Ranch near Cimarron, N.M. but will stop en route at the Hearst Castle and Disneyland."

Portland Oregonian

In Troop 51 in those days
you put your red name button on the new Official beanie
& went off to Camp Royaneh in trucks. Smoked basket reeds.
Drank bug juice. Got poison oak & a sunburn. Wrote Mom for
clean underwear & hunting knife just like Jack's. Or maybe got bored with the whole MaryAnn, came home early & put on
old cords
to see some Westerns.

Panning for gold in Cimarron
based on universality of the acquisitive instinct
& therefore political
& Open to Question.

Disneyland I enjoyed
but I was an Adult
functioning that day as an independent intoxicated unit
& knew what to look for. But Disneyland: the Outdoors?
Open to Question.

Hearst Castle we vote to table until next meeting.

What I see is a bunch of fake sunshine.
Sammy Davis, Jr. might as well try Othello (Or Rockefeller, Lear.)
Put me in there, we'd go through the Southwest picking beer cans
out of mountain streams. Milk some goats, get tanked on bug
juice, miss a few mountains by inches

then hot-foot some of them Spanish magistrates

Roger Pfingston

Waiting for Nighthawks in Illinois

"Come out and watch the nighthawks fly,"
he said, and I did, having never seen one.
"Now those are chimney swifts there,
the nighthawk will climb much higher
and then suddenly dive hard and straight
for three or four seconds. Damndest thing
you ever saw if you've never seen it,
and even if you have it's worth sitting for.
I'm out here most every night, and some nights,
if we're out late, we come home
and hear them up there making a noise
like a buzzer going off and we know it's nighthawks."

A full moon rose from behind a neighbor's tree
over Hoopeston, "sweet corn capital of the world."
From the back porch we watched and waited
as the swifts played overhead like a circus act.
Now and then a few dropped down the chimney
on the old library next door.

"They'll be up there soon," he said,
"and it's a pretty sight. You wait and see."

I believed him, and lit another cigar.

About the Cows

About the cows, they would not stay
as Hayflick warned, having been spooked
by something less appreciative of cows
than he or I. Dogs perhaps, or kids
on trail bikes. "Even neighbors, faces more
familiar than yours," he said, "are not enough
to make them keep their shade. They'll up
and move away as you approach, and cameras
are not something they understand."

But I thought I would try, having gone
to the trouble of driving down the road,
and no sooner had I stepped over the low
wire fence than they began to eye me
as if I were a butcher. Several heaved
their great bulk up on all fours, and as I
raised the camera it was as Hayflick said.

Nevertheless, I have this photograph,
this one, that glows with the soft light
of cows drifting off at evening time,
some looking back suspiciously
as they crowd each other toward the woods
where Stoutes Creek flows past the quarry.

Roger Pfingston

Frank Lamont Phillips

A special moment

A special moment
is the soul's release

We would all fly free
if we but had
wings

A special moment
captured in the heart
to be remembered
long

to be stored in
family Bibles
where
written poorly
on a single page
it is noted
that

"Once we was slaves"

Judy Ray

Felix Pollak

Widow

"Our life together," she says,
and her voice breaks.
All around, a desert of stones,
grey sarcophagi for the living
reaching into a smoky sky. Her voice,
a tremolo of retrospective visions,
transforms the stonescape into a
flowering garden, leading to the beach.
"Our life together," she says,
her voice breaking into song.

His sardonic counterpoint is not
in earshot now, his half-smile
out of sight. A pun, incognito,
dies on the carpet. His silence
is audible only to few. She covers it,
quoting him freely — a filter-tipped
replay that bears her out.
"Our life together," she trills.

Her words, endowed by faith, move
mountains and mausoleums. She is not choosy
as to her confidants — any pair of
willing ears will do. Naturally, there were
grievances, he was not easy. Of course
there were spats. But even Adam and Eve,
she suspects, had those. Yet would you
denigrate the sun because of sunspots?
"Oh, our life together," she sighs.

If there are whisperings of guilt,
they're drowned in the song of the brook
that winds its way through evergreens.
And nightmares? Lightning flashes in the wee
hours illuminating the barren structures that
contained her bed and a cold grave? If so,
they have no witnesses — not even herself
the morning after. Nor will her dreams
have witnesses again, she vows, for quite some time
to come. "Remember our life together," she whispers,
as she falls asleep.

David Posner

Mourningsong for Anne

You signed yourself into the loony bin so often
It was like signing the hotel register—
Not a particularly elegant hotel—
Full of polite transients and a few permanents
Who sat futile as potted palms fading into the TV
In the old-fashioned foyer that always reminded you of home.
There were moments, peering out the barred window of your fourth
floor suite
When nevertheless you could see between the reflections of headlights,
Nightclub blinkers, and the neon from the flowershop at the corner,
A flawless glowing of stars in a full heaven.
Then you would telephone your daughters to send them your love;
Chainsmoke, revising two lines eighty-six times;
Or open up the cupboard where your new dress hung,
Try it on in the mirror: black
But chic, I can hear you saying.
Sometimes, long past visiting hours,
A message in a strange handwriting (not your doctor's)
Got slipped noiselessly under the door:
I suppose, by one of those tall, dark, handsome
Gentlemen the Victorians were so crazy about.

Alan Proctor

At Night

Something steps from leaf to leaf
leans against the house and shakes me,
my wife wakes also. She is wondering
what I see in poetry, in bed like this
with my notebook. "Alan?"
I am thinking about the cannisters of nerve gas
honeycombed outside Salt Lake City.

Paul Ramsey

On the Porch of the Antique Dealer

The stopped clocks
Shine
In the sun.

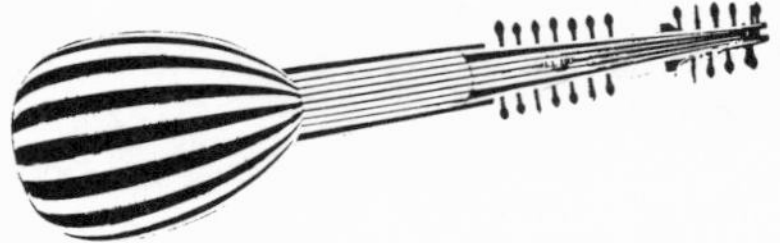

Rush Rankin

The Woman Who Combed

She combed her long hair at the window,
where the wall of the city
faced fields of white stones, and smiled

as though he touched her
past lovers, by slipping
into her while she combed
her long hair at the window.

In the distance near
the river lay a crippled horse.
A dazed courier could be seen
limping toward the horizon.

She combed her long hair
at the window as a signal
to the invaders, who were stunned

by the suicide
of a large man and surprised
that children watched from the trees.

Julian Lee Rayford

Junkyards

You take any junkyard
you will see it is filled
with symbols of progress
remarkable things discarded

What civilization went ahead on
all its onward-impelling implements
are given over the junkyards
to rust

The supreme implement, the wheel
is conspicuous in the junkyards

The axles and the levers
the cogs and the flywheels
all the parts of dynamos
all the parts of motors
rusting

Carl Rakosi

The Avocado Pit

a complete earth
hard as stone
the size of a plum
Pompeian red,
darkened and faded
like an old Roman mural
from the bath house
of Menander,
golden brown
with delicate veins
as if the earth
had cracked with age
or we were looking
at the rivers
from a satellite.

The China Policy

Of all the old times
I'll take Chinese poetry.
A man could loll under a hemlock tree then
and muse,
and nature be
as wood to carpenters,
a grouse ambling by,
a sparrow hopping . . .
nothing was of greater consequence . . .
such sweetness flowing
as through a membrane through his limbs
the universe turned
into a poet's enclave,
the great society
where simplicity is character
and character the common tongue,
the representative of man.

In those corrupt, bitter times
the most obscure clerk
could attain clarity
from these poems,
and his nature,
and change into a superior man
of exquisite modesty
by simply looking at a heron crossing a stream.

The Vow

Matter,
with this look
I wed thee
and become
thy very
attribute.
I shall
be thy faithful
spouse,
true
to thy nature,
for I love
thee
more than Durer
loved a seaweed.

David Ray

Extreme Unction In Pa.

No, not the last *Last Supper*, and yet
for the sake of the world I mumbled all
the holy poems I knew. They too
were dying. Outside the silver diner
rain fell and fell, and from the South
came wind that bore the glowing mask,
danced the silly saffron masque of hell.
And though I dreaded walking out,
inhaling tiny drifts from Satan's mills
that stood upon the earth like pots
of clay, turned on a loving wheel,
I'd try to tip my hat to the waitress
to keep her calm. *Go down gentle*,
I hoped to say, stay still upon your stools,
all you chubby drivers, innocent and hungry,
and feathered ladies on some worldly journey.
The sky went dark. Trees were trembling.
We had our share of cobalt blue,
but heavy lead had followed, and iodine
like that blind Homer kicked upon the shore, seaweed.

The Jogger: Denver to Kansas City

Midway, he paces the cheap hotel room,
dried out from its clanking radiator.
He'll pace, smoke, and sleep fitfully all day,
a very picture of tired, restless gloom,
and at night take the Greyhound bus on for
another hundred miles or more. They'll say
he jogged all through Kansas, and hand him
the silver trophy. In the always dim
light of his carpet shop, they'll urge some more
details from him, as if he'd been at war.
"I tell you," he scoffs, "there's not much to say.
It's very desolate out there. I ran mostly
at night. I saw no one. It was ghostly."
And he thinks of that secret room, half-way.

Judy Ray

Rose Bay Willow Herb

The willow herb, the
rose bay willow herb,
sweeps woods and commons
with pink sunset stripes.
It rises from black
aftermath of fire
that crackled through thick
undergrowth of trees.
Even after war
it flourishes in
empty lots, in bomb
craters, and like a
phoenix of flora
rises tall and wild,
true fireweed, indeed.
Should the air it spikes,
water it drinks, ash
it grows from become
radioactive,
aftermath of a
great folly, perhaps
the willow herb, the
rose bay willow herb,
will still grow wild with
pink sunset stripes and
bloom abundantly.
But who will there be
of our coughing, skin-
flaking, misshapen
kind to perceive a
symbol of hope? And
perhaps the only
phoenix to arise
from that blind folly
will be some tiny
flung molecule of
untainted earth with
no memory of
tall willow herb, wild
rose bay willow herb.

Lloyd J. Reynolds

WEATHERGRAMS are poems of about ten words. They are written on narrow strips of kraft paper cut from used grocery store bags. They are hung on bushes or trees in gardens, parks, or along mountain trails.

Usually seasonal, they are left out between the solstice and equinox or between equinox and solstice— or longer. The name means weather-writing, & they are only potential until sun, wind, rain, & possibly ice, frost and snow have rubricated them. Left out long enough, they resemble ragged, faded leaves or material cut from a wasp's nest.

Written in acrylic polymer vermilion & waterproof India ink, the script will outlast the paper. One was weathered into a rag of paper & frayed string and was woven into a robin's nest.

Similar to Japanese *tanzaku*, the weathergram, however, had an independent origin. The influences of Haiku poetry and Zen Buddhist thought are sometimes apparent, but weathergrams are quite Western and not pseudo-Oriental.

Weathergrams are neither didactic nor epigrammatic. Similies are avoided. William Carlos Williams' "No idea but in things." That's IT! But the things are simultaneously things and not-things. Consider "An inch of puddle reflects miles of sky." Or this spontaneous comment on a blizzard: "It's white, even between the snowflakes." And these, composed by high school students in Tacoma: "Brushing the bough, my body bends." And "We run laughing down the dry creek bed."

Other examples: Every puddle finds its own moon. ¢ Sunlight under dark soil comes up dandelions. ¢ Buttercups next snow —so *that's* what winter's been up to! ¢ Touching your bark to the tree's skin. ¢ The leaves falling, sky moves in between the branches.

Lacking development, can it be called a poem? If not, all right— just call it a weathergram.

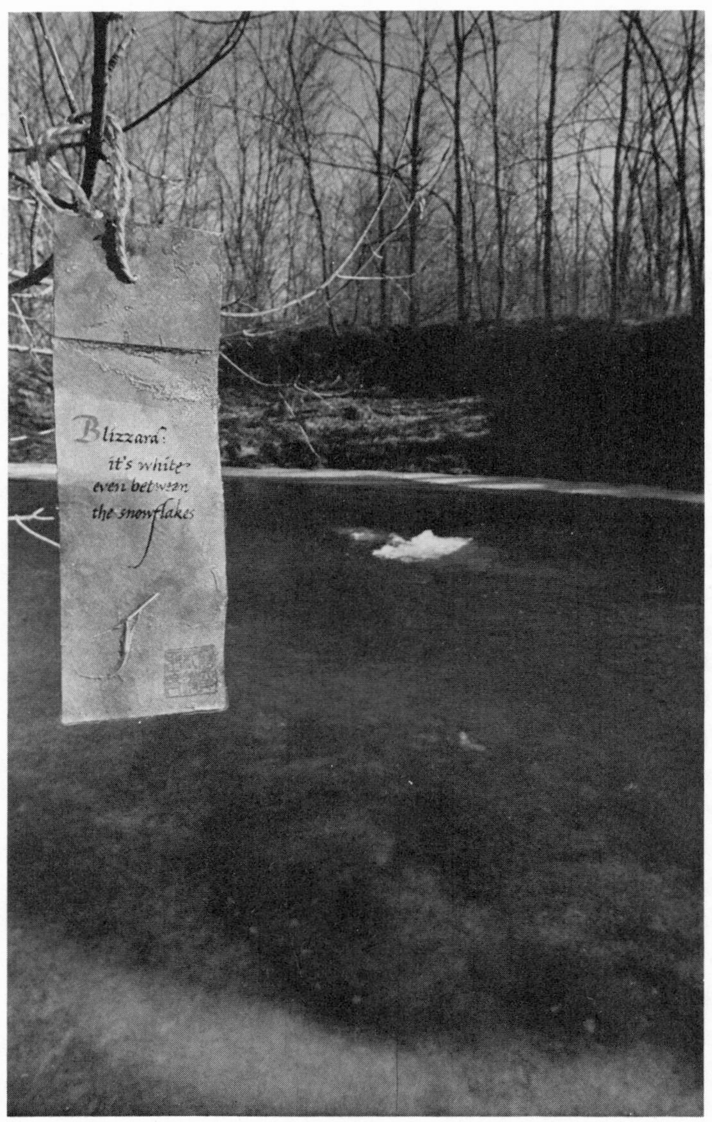
Blizzard:
it's white
even between
the snowflakes

Bob Barrett

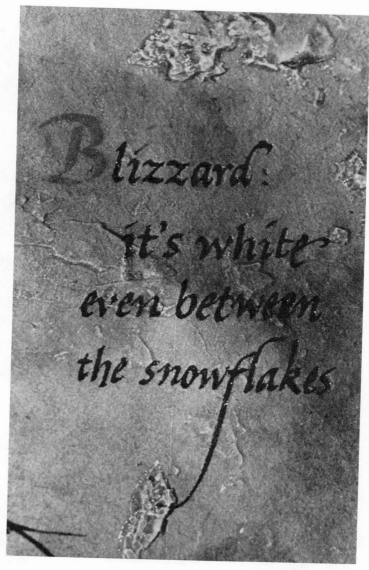

Bob Barrett

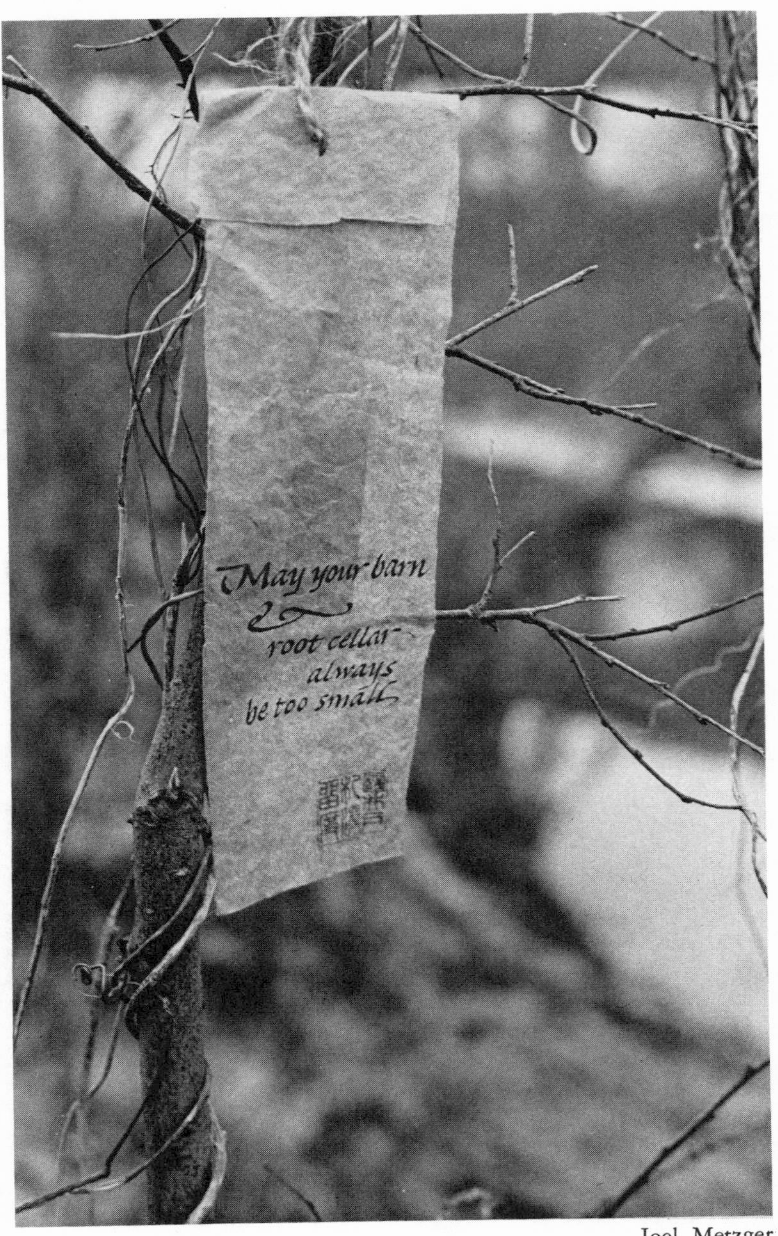
May your barn
&
root cellar
always
be too small

Joel Metzger

John C. Rezmerski

Sonship

The end of October after a rain.
My father complains
that standards are not uniform
for pipes and sewers from town to town.
Complains loudly to local officials
with vests and important hats
and folded arms and gold teeth.
Small as I am, I try to agree
by not shivering—
after all he is my father.
It is difficult
to argue our case in the streets,
full of cracks and holes as they are.
People throw chunks of coal at us,
hard coal that shines colors in the sun,
arcing down at our heads
like dud bombs.
I am surprised they could disrespect
the old man like that,
and wish I could stop ducking and watch
them clap and laugh at our dancing and shouting.

Raymond Roseliep

When I was Nine

Father's locking up our house,
darkness paws the town.
In my coffin I can hear
hands reaching down.

Mother puts away her thread
till another sunrise.
The lid creaks open at a word
from burning eyes.

House grows quiet as an old
remembered snuff of pain.
We ride against the nighttime's
sweet tooth of rain.

Farewell, Father and your key,
Mother and your floss.
No garlic wreath can catch me,
nor your cold, cold cross.

Harry Roskolenko

Waiting for God

(from Baguio Poems)

The things that were not spiritual,
Like ordering shirts, jacket—buying
The hands of others, to sew up my future;
To have a drink at the bar in my hotel,
To ask a girl to come up and massage
My back, neck, thighs, all my essences . . .
And she praised my age; I still have hair,
That young skin, and she did not know
Why I had come to see a Healer named Placido.

When I asked what she thought, she thought
That it was good that I had come to Baguio;
To feel her hands — and she healed me of nothing;
Massage hands, hands for middle-age's fornication;
And when she did not massage, she barbered my hair;
A maid for all things not always of the spirit;
That it was good that I had come to Baguio,
To see her and a Healer named Placido.

Come Unto Us Who Are . . . Laden

The names, the people, the times . . . they
Said *I/Thou* . . . and I hear the dogs barking;
It Is The Year Of Our . . . and all of them said again,
Come Unto . . . it is the hour that defines the hour;
Time/ Split . . . and how many Infinities can we possess?
We Live But . . . let us light all the blacker candles,
But there are no colors, hues, races anymore;
There is only "the power of the enigmatic hour . . ."
And every philosophy undoes itself within itself;
And the faces of children and their voices — come,
As the sun comes, the seasons go . . . and we remain
To listen to dogs barking; it is a dog's life
Of bones, meat, drink, blood, cities, fields, streams . . .
Time, *Thou*, *Split*, *Colors*, *Earth*, *Sun* . . . and *We* remain.

Symbols

All those words that I've used for sixty-eight years,
And what shall I remember of my earlier "language of love"?
Discordant, exhultant, moon-bolted, words of energy,
"Your green eyes, how much like the sea — they are";
All those younger words . . . *your brown-nippled breasts*,
When my language was proper, polite, youth-seized,
When my words were like my hands *touching you gently*,
Your thighs deranging all my fluid devastations;
All those years — *the windless sailing of the heart*;
And during the war's terror 33 years ago—
"In yesterday's uniform we glimpse tomorrow's face."

In love there is every drama of disaster,
The act of one and one becoming two and two,
Deflections on windy streets on stumbling feet,
And birds in clusters of flight suddenly echoing . . .
What games are they playing now with my eyes?

All those words of stress, strain, tears and love;
Where have they gone in my ambushing damnations?
I cannot recall the changes of her redder hair . . .
Nor the depth of her large-eyed interior surprise,
The propulsions of earlier morals, one week's infinities;
Symbols, games, radiant, red, blonde, loving — so long ago.

Larry Rubin

Registered at the Bordello Hotel (Vienna)

You hand me my key with a smile like a starched sheet
I wait for the lift with eyes averted from the halls
The silence is a secret known to flies and gods
The twenty-seven steps to my room
I walk past doors locked against my wildly growing hands
The smell of human dust sifts through the crevices
With laughter echoed in coiled twangs—
I throw the bolt and hide
All night the stars consult about my case

By dawn all rooms are empty
Between my stainless sheets
I sleep in the sweat of a single heart

Vern Rutsala

Pursuit

And now I follow my father
For three years
Living on crackers
Drinking from puddles
I bide my time
Watching
As he shadows the three
Who beat hell out of him
Behind Finn Hall
It is my job
I must do it right
Salty crackers biting
The sores on my tongue
Winter turning my feet
To stumps
But I hang on
As one by one
He catches them
And makes them pay

Ralph Salisbury

A Halo

In somebody's shoes some Gypsies war-dance water to their Roman tower
Moors wrecked and clouds sifting like flour over Friday fish
Down from the Malaga hills become the smoke of Great Grandad's
Stockade sunset in it a halo pink

Gibraltar pales to my father's pipe-puff drifting above the white
Capped waves of uncut Christmas trees the day the blood of a fox
Made snow seem sunset surf

More vivid than fur chicken-fat sleeked a halo of red widened
Pink turning red and a further pink appearing as air which haiku
Had shaped is said to have spread from Hiroshima and still—
As a home smashed bones of Romans moulder under genes in the marrow
Powdered asunder an asteroid belt of babies— still as stone
Again dims pink spreads from red spreading from red and spreads
And spreads against the dark

Andrew Salkey

Postcard from London, 23. 10. 1972

For John La Rose

When our brothers,
yours from Trinidad,
mine from Jamaica,
passed through,
the other day
from Port of Spain
and Kingston,
they looked beaten
by prosperity,
switched out
by property
and profit.

We wanted, badly,
to stop them,
in their pain,
and ask them
to look again
at themselves
and the hope of change.

But they seemed
in a hurry,
and seemed so right!
Instead,
we talked to each other.

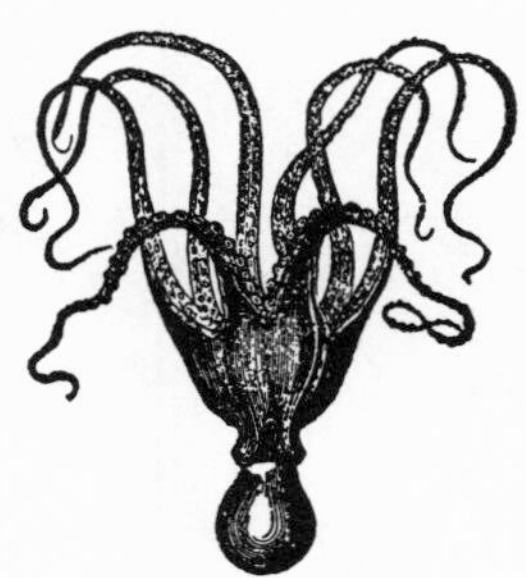

Ted Schaefer

The Parents-Without-Partners Picnic

Cosmos Park, Columbia, Missouri

At Cosmo
the sky is swarming with color
"just like finger-
paint before it dries."
The kids are skinny, sure
of themselves
in sneakers—blue rubber
mated to red—noisily
assaulting a hub
of pipes
with mindless bravado.
Our jokes are *Caveat Emptor.*
Cold chicken in tinfoil,
bakery pie,
as if to prove
we're only good in bed.
Norma shoplifts.
We laugh about the
K-Mart Blue Light Specials.
Allen says he takes too many pills.
Dick supports
a "bearded manifesto" from the college
in his $50,000 home. It hurts
to see them, naked,
in the pool.
Lucille's husband, she said,
came home from the army base waving
a pistol at her head. Mindy
knew when she heard the power-mower stall.
And Vietnam—
Little Tammy doesn't understand.
Jesse does. He says
his father's buried under
the White House.
Therapy taught Susan (pert
and buxom in a yellow pantsuit)
the value of confession: "Frankly,
in a way,

I almost envy you widows . . . "
A sudden chill.
Most of us
have taken up smoking again,
our cigarettes so crazy in the dark.

Anxiety Pastorale

A Nazi in a Zeppelin
has anchored,
low,
between the stars and rows of corn.
We swallow our fear.
Up there
what's he thinking?
Tonight there's death on a neighboring farm,
its windows suddenly gold.

James Schevill

The Necessity of Rejection

Another rejection. What ecstasy.
Another blow to Ego and to Eros.
My body shakes with the will to endure.

A Lesson in Hammocks

At the Montejo Palace in Merida
Built by a Spanish Conquistador
After Cortes's conquest of Mexico,
The mestizo guide, cigar in hand,
Takes off in a joyful hammock swing
Demonstrating the art of tropical sleep,
How to hover free from bugs and scorpions.
With glee he invites the American ladies
To open the hammock as wide as possible.
Gingerly they pull it out like a fleshly fan.
"What do you see, ladies, what do you see?"
"A very large hammock, that's what we see."
"Dear ladies, it's a matrimonial hammock for love."
Puffing his cigar with a teacher's delight
The guide flies up and down in the hammock,
His cigar on fire for the sensual life.

Dennis Schmitz

Adolescence

this dream won't fit
a parent's
interrupted face nor the prodigal

dead firemen hug
to the used breath of the oxy-mask
hoping the face will age

into the mask
our senses make. smoke kills
the youngest at their

desks, hands folded
over graffiti pubic
drawings or answers to older

quizzes. others know
fire by instinct or as they fall
on one another smothered

at the exit:
the door which always opens
inward, door a friend's body

will block
forcing boy & girl to lie
down together untaught

in the adjacent dark.

Grace Schulman

Epithalamion

Look there! *The Lovers*
in the Flowers.
Chagall's lovers, forever
ungoverned by gravity,
surface the air
like water, or
lean on lilacs
above a moon,
over the distant
fragment of a castle.
Is it fantasy? Hands,
faces, arms
are real, but made
of smoke: sometimes
in wind,
it skims the earth
but always rises.

Harvey Shapiro

1976

Vision floats
Over the death camps.
That stink. Till the end
Of history. Not soteriology
Or the American sublime
Can raise man up,
Magnified and sanctified.
The fallen sparks,
Husks, on the street corners,
In the streets.

Incident

Tremendous pleasure lurking in my skin.
You stretch, your small breasts announcing,
This is the beginning. If we were to lie together,
I would have to tell you my long story.
Slowly I begin to rehearse it.

Father and Sons

If you tell them something truthful
About themselves or about life,
Coming across it
In the middle of a rambling discourse,
How solemn their faces grow.

Morty Sklar

Poem to the Sun

You want to sit here and write a poem,
here in Rossi's Cafe on Gilbert,
main drag trucks early a.m.
across from end of March puddle empty lots
across from sun

You want to sit across from empty puddle lots,
sun hop skip and jump from
rooftop shingle to puddle to semi windshield
shatter, in the dust diffused in window,
home fries eggs sunnyside grease air in Rossi's,
ninety-three million miles

        beamed down, twenty-five feet from a
puddle, a puddle, ye gads, ninety-three
million miles to a puddle, no, not yet
O Great Starship, don't beam me
back

        . . . the snow
has just melted here,
light spreading like a cosmic *good* virus,
glinting off auburn coffee, splashed on
the floor tossed around in mop
with radio wave mix from shelf
transistor

        . . . You want to sit here,
a living crystal receiver, here,
goddamn,
   40 billion trillion miles from nowhere,

next to a puddle,
next to the sun.

Robert Slater

The Survivors

We remember now
grandmothers who had
children by the litter.

Letters are sent
as far away as
Oregon in search

of a father.
The survivors are
all but forgotten:

the anonymous ones
the ones we inspired
the ones we pestered.

The sides are chosen.
The forces aligned.
Our work is done.

We who in the beginning
were such an influence
are left to mind the fences.

Survival Kit

These lines
Are the truth.
Believe them.

The survival manuals
Are all wrong.

The liberation lies
Somewhere between
These veins
And those latitudes.

A. G. Sobin

Greeting Descendants

"Someday you may have to draw
your water by hand from wells . . . "

From all my ancestors
how little has come to me;

along a line of grey faces
curving slowly to the east
I am passed on like a stick.

I may pass you by at night
curving east in a fog
only a sound over cobblestones
like something on wheels

or come to you perhaps
hand over hand, a white look
in the bottom of a pail.

Roger Pfingston

William Stafford

For a Plaque on the Door of an Isolated House

Someone Here, listen to your pulse and
breathing. These are loud, Someone
Here. These make a house tremble.
A long bridge has found this moment;
many birds came over in the night
and carried a message no one could
read. Remember a friend, this hour
in your life. There will be storms;
there will be prizes and hurts. There will be
nights when you swing out over the deep.
But there are little rooms in your life like
this pause at the door, Someone Here.

Look

From my head this bubble labeled "Love"
goes up. It is in color, like a balloon. I am
thinking it. And my hair is crowded like that
often. I remember streams of bubbles
when I walk—they go bouncing off through the trees.
And once my neck got stretched on Main by a big
ballooning thought when the mayor's daughter suddenly
turned and took me for someone else. This
bend when I listen, even today, is that romance
that flared and went out so fast that no one knew.
Any time, any time, big ideas come along.
This bubble here is always ready, for you.

Surviving a Poetry Circuit

My name is Old Mortality—mine is the hand
that carves the tombstones all over the land.

When you talk, I listen. My ears are keen—
not for what you say, but for what the lies may mean.

If you look away when those around you are hurt,
I bend for my chisel and pick it up from the dirt,

And for every evil you do I cut one more line
across the face of a rock at the end of time.

To make all clean and clear, I tap on your tombstone,
lest moss take all our names when Old Mortality's gone.

In the Morning All Over

High there in our grove the little birds
chirp, sweeping up their rooms, their best
wall the wind, branches for the rest, now and then
a song just to hold the walls up
while the legs pump those hollow little bones.

Two philosophers come to dissect a sparrow,
looking for the real. First they strip
the feathers, then they rip the skin . . . the blood—
gleefully they find those little bones: hollow.
Two philosophers. They stare through the air.

Now let's have a song, just to hold the walls up:
Many ways to go, the best wall is the wind.

Magic Lantern

Here is that far, deep country I've
told you about. Here's lightning—then
birch trees picketing miles of burnt-over
upland, and one tree tracing with its roots
a charcoal river system deep in the earth
where the hot bolt followed everything alive
into cracks in the rock.

This tree has a carved heart. This last
is a negative I hold. It looks like
a map of the Yukon with grizzlies
tugging the corners and Eskimoes running
from a blue north wind.
Now I put the magic lantern away.
Some other day we'll have lightning again.

The Mountain That Got Little

Hidden far somewhere trembling with
fear, there is a mountain, somewhere there,
a mountain that got little, till one day it was
gone—it couldn't stand being
laughed at: it put its little cap
on and slipped away.

That was up in Alaska, where a mountain or
so would hardly be missed.
But here in our house we always would
know if there was a mountain,
no matter how little it is.

Drummer Boy

An army in the dust
   raised by
the wind along the road
   into the pasture
guided by moments, every
   wave, every screaming
gust, headlong across the open—

"Listen, you at home, you
   being careful:
I am someone forgotten.
   If a wind pats
your coat, that is my story,
   how I turn,
the trouble in my life.

"But that's gone now—
   I skip in the gravel.
All that I did has turned into this song."

Friend Who Never Came

It has not been given me to have a friend
so steady the world becomes an incident
and all else leads us both to that event
when glances cross while two fates depend.
It has not been given. A life will end
somewhere at random, silent of rest, silent
that might have whispered another world and bent
this one around us. Here is my farewell, friend
who never came: There was a morning in June,
when I was young, and a family just from the farm
parked by our yard, not knowing what to do.
The daughter trembling lay—"Sunstroke last noon,"
they said. They soothed her, drove slowly on. The harm
had been in her eyes. They rolled, once—"I was for you."

Sometimes in the sun today I glimpse that world in the blue.

Stephen Stepanchev

Autumn Song

Feeling sick, I take my morning walk.
Luis, the porter, is sweeping red maple leaves
Off the sidewalk with a broom.
A brown voice behind me is singing the blues.

Farther on, I see a boy blowing soap bubbles
In the air, little iridescent balloons.
Near him, under a tree, a bench of happy pensioners
Shakes with laughter in the speckled light of pale
Oak leaves. What's their secret?

I stare at rooftop television aerials
And see them as storks standing on long, elegant legs.

I remember last summer's swarm of wasps
Which flew in suddenly
And killed the cicadas and laid eggs in their corpses.

Thousands of new selves
Rose joyously out of those deaths.

Judy Ray

Bert Stern

Looking For a Home

He drove to Terre Haute
After fighting three hours
With his wife on a Saturday night
Rage and whorehouses
His headlights
And cats'-eyes

In the first bar
He quarreled with drunks
About whatever came along
Fat ladies in purple slacks
Moved among tables
Like dogs on business

Later the barmaid
Stopped his beer when he said shit
He thought of San Francisco
But drove home
Turning the headlights
Off from time to time

To watch the October leaves
In the dark

Robert Stewart

Ballet Under The Stars

Now, the people are getting their art
warming this park hillside,
behind a pine tree somewhere, Basho
mourns the rising souls of crickets

we could be in Athens now, trees
all we see—sirens coming through
the leaves and knot holes
squirrel nests flashing red

last week beside the swan lagoon
two girls danced beneath a knife
no one announced the event
or heard the quick crescendo

applause rises with the arabesque
silent drama edging us together
safe now: every bug that can fly
is down at the spotlight.

The Plumber Arrives At Three Mile Island

A plumber's price is high because he uses
equipment that can channel what diffuses—
since heavy duty's standard on some jobs,
and augers, threaders, clamps and come-alongs
can bring our flooded dreams another turn.
Unless a plumber has somewhere to stand
he'll wade right in among the toilet fish
and fumble with the break below the wastes,
among those places we will not admit,
where all our bright ideas turn to shit.
But now the whole trade's dirty—used to be
just septic tanks and sewers; it used to be
a plumber always had a place to wash
when he was through to tally up the costs.

Ann Struthers

Watching the Out-door Movie Show

On summer Saturday nights in Persia, Iowa, I saw
the Lone Ranger and Tonto and the great white horse
Silver while overhead in the coffee sky
a meteor shower began. Wild horses
of the West galloped across the screen becoming stars
shooting toward the edge of the universe. I rode
the leader his flaming mane throwing
off sparks as we whistled through the wind
across the prairies of ennui into the forested
foothills down the forbidden canyons.

Even now the horses of the stars
canter, early on Sunday mornings.

Martha Maverick

Lucien Stryk

Farmer

Seasons waiting the miracle,
dawn after dawn framing
the landscape in his eyes:

bound tight as wheat, packed
hard as dirt. Made shrewd
by soil and weather, through

the channel of his bones
shift ways of animals,
their matings twist his dreams.

While night-fields quicken,
shadows slanting right, then left
across the moonlit furrows,

he shelters in the farmhouse
merged with trees, a skin of wood,
as much the earth's as his.

LUCIEN STRYK

Zen Poems, After Shinkichi Takahashi

Afternoon

My hair's falling fast—
this afternoon
I'm off to Asia Minor.

Downy Hair

Charmed by a girl's soft ears,
I piled up leaves and burnt them.

How innocent her face
in rising smoke—I longed

to roam the spiral of those ears,
but she clung stiffly

to the tramcar strap, downy
hair fragrant with leafsmoke.

Haiku from the Japanese Masters translated.

Fish shop—
how cold the lips
of the salted bream.
BASHO

Moor:
point my horse
where birds sing.
BASHO

Plum-viewing:
in the gay quarter
sashes are chosen.
BUSON

No need to cling
to things
floating frog.
JOSO

by Lucien Stryk and Takashi Ikemoto

These branches
were the first to bud—
falling blossoms.

JOSO

Seaweed
between rocks—
forgotten tides.

KITO

Things long forgotten—
pot where a flower blooms,
this spring day.

SHIKI

Even in my village
now, I sleep
like a traveler.

KYORAI

David Swanger

Probity

The children ask questions;
they are scientists of nouns.
Luckily I have answers.

Moon: the end of a hollow bone.
Sun: a gold tooth in a big grin.
Death: a weed you can't pull.

The children suspect something.
Already they have plans to grow
umbrellas under the side porch.

John Tagliabue

just a few scenes from an autobiography

I eat noodles with the Emperor's brother
in a school basement, he tells me about baseball,
I tell him about Gagaku

I translate the sounds of a cricket
with a musician or elf then
I become the cricket

I go to the moon with my mother
and we weep there for all the ashes
and for all the dead in all the wars

I look at student essays by the millions
and put scribbles meaning awkward by some words
I prepare lectures for over 30 years

I listen to messages from all things that
sooner or later are speaking directly to me
and my wife and I travel in love

Archilochos:

" . . . Keep some measure in your joy—
or in your sadness during / crisis
that you may understand man's up-and-down life."

O yes   O yes
We've lived long enough to know how true that is,
        up and down, up and down,
many deep depressions, — but then again those
        curves like a woman's breasts!
The good life returns to us in perfect weather or
        perfect pleasure
        nipples showing.

Debussy And Proust

The Customs Seal on my travel bag
        almost faded,
        looking like a miniature of an old map,
the old vaccination mark on my left arm almost faded,
        the dim moon in the morning sky,
        the memory of so many days
        and nights and flowers come
        and gone almost faded;
before you go, map of God on the fading body of the dancer,
mark of acceptance by the international officer,
        ancient body of an insect on a leaf,
        before you go I want to just
        mention you, repeat your names,
        say the alphabet from A to Z,
want to say as long as I can remember I will
        murmur prayers and the reverence
        of things past.

Stephen Tapscott

Parable: November

How happy the red
harvest precede
the winter dead
so firmly.

so inevitably
organized. surely
some broader
than ours hand shepherds

these suite
regularities, that hand
that wraps
the onions

specifically, stashed
in the burlap
sack beside the fragrant apple
bushel under my back stoop!

Judy Ray

James Tate

Same Tits

It was one of those kind of days. I was walking down the St.
and this poster glassed in a theater billboard caught my eye.
A Really gorgeous set of tits. It was noon, hot as hell
outside. So I said what the hell, paid my 2.50 and went
in. Got a seat all by myself right in the middle. The
curtain opens: there's the same poster by itself in the
middle of the stage. I sat there sweating. Finally
decided to get the hell out of there. It was still noon,
hot as hell outside.

John Taylor

End of the Line

This is the end of the line.
You get out, trying to read the name
Of the station under the one light,
But it is another alphabet
Than the one you learned by heart,
And the wind out of all those miles
Of darkness behind the station
Is another wind. Still, the stars are the same,
And you turn up your collar, settle your pack,
And start. The agent stares inside his window;
You wave, shout a word in his language
As you cross the platform and step out
Into the surf-sound of grass
And start walking. The Dipper's clouded,
But there's Cassiopeia, so you know
Which way to go, and you feel like walking
After so long on the train. There's moonlight
Enough, there's the grass rising and falling,
And when you get tired, there's your bag,
And when you wake up, there's the map.
End of the line? There's only one end
Of the line: keep moving till then.

Roses Gone Wild

Where is my roof that kept out the rain?
Where are my walls that kept out the wind?
Where is my walk that I walked upon?
Where is the hole to show they are gone?
Far away, far away,
Far and far and far away
Wind cries in roses gone wild.

Where is my wife who loved me so long?
Where is the bed which kept us both warm?
Where are our children and how do they live?
Where is the water kept in a sieve?
Far away, far away,
Far and far and far away
Wind cries in roses gone wild.

Where is the money I earned for our bread?
Where is the city I made it all in?
Where is the flag that flew over it all?
Where is an echo ever so small?
Far away, far away,
Far and far and far away
Wind cries in roses gone wild.

The Mill

Let's hug our grudges, love
The toad the carver tucked in among angels,
Admire the cleft the *shiela-na-gig* demands
We admire. How often we save

Ourselves by demanding stone
For bread. To most this must be mystery
Who do not know the millstone or the mill
Or what it grinds for grain.

Let's take for our emblem
The dead cicada clinging to the screen;
It has been months, in spite of how the wind
Has beaten its dumb drum.

Virginia R. Terris

Drinking

We are drinking from one another
as if we were plants in the same jungle
where rain is continually falling.

Bending into one another
our leaves rustle in the wet silences
growing and turning upward
where green light seeps
around the wings of birds
crying against the sky

our roots knotting themselves
in that dark world
that allows us our drunkenness.

Roger Pfingston

Phyllis Thompson

The Wind of the Cliff Ka Hea

At blackest night to come alone in rain.
Never less hard than before or any safer,
But I will find you and speak with you
    Out of nothing.

There is no one here. I cannot sing for myself.
How shall I free the body the words need?
I uncover, as I would to you,
    Shoulder, breast, belly, and thigh.

Under my bare feet the unshaken cliff, fixed in the ocean.
The fire-striking, prised-apart sky beyond stretch of my arms.
The stave of my body raked by rain as I wait for the wind
    That rises from nothing.

I have never known such purity of cold
As swirls inside this cliff, beginning to quiver now
As the wind collects what is lost still
    In thick night.

A soft bite, a shivering, a leap, a ghostly air
Rising where you are.
A night wind blowing time around
    Some form of life.
And I sink into rifts in your memory's sleep.
Tenderly falling I slip into your dream's abyss
A wind shaken out endlessly endlessly seeking you
    To bring you here.
From whatever world you live in
    To bring you here.

Adrift in the strong air that is
Speaking the hidden things
I have, not knowing, needed,
My call passes down
Into silence, into peace, into morning
At the base of the cliff.

Jim Trifilio

Hokkaido

On the island of Hokkaido
the women are sitting
at rosewood tables,
heels set firmly in buttocks,
molding ricecakes.
The old man is fixing squid.
His sons are neck deep
in boiling water
down from Mt. Tarumae.
The children are rocking sole
to sole:
"Let us ride on a sailboat,
let us sail on the ocean."
A handful of
sand a handful
of sand a
handful of sand
and the mound falls down.
The salmon will move next day
through one gate in the fence
stretched across Mukawa River
where quick hands will slip
fingers in redpetal gills;
flipped in baskets.
A bear cub sits for the carver
who takes him into the tree
and is set at the corner
of the cooking pit
in the home of his eldest son.
The early dew grows on bamboo mats,
forgotten,
left outside to dry from
the night before.
Families sleep cousin by uncle, wife by son,
sister by sister around the fire
that no one watches go out.

Melvin B. Tolson

Sootie Joe

The years had rubbed out his youth,
But his fellows ranked him still
As a chimney-sweep without a peer . . .
Whether he raced a weighted corset
Up and down the throat of a freakish flue,
Or, from a chair of rope,
His eyes goggled and his mouth veiled,
He wielded his scraping knife
Through the walled-in darkness.

The soot from ancient chimneys
Had wormed itself into his face and hands.
The four winds had belabored the grime on him.
The sun had trifled with his ebony skin
And left ashen spots.

Sometimes Sootie Joe's wealthy customers
Heard him singing a song that gave them pause:

I's a chimney-sweeper, a chimney-sweeper,
I's black as the blackest night.
I's a chimney-sweeper, a chimney-sweeper,
And the world don't treat me right.
But somebody hasta black hisself
For somebody else to stay white.

Peg Leg Snelson

Peg Leg Snelson
Is strutting his stuff at the Harlem Club.
I saw him stop the show on Broadway
In the *Dark Town Scandals of 1929.*
He can tap out the intricate rhythms
Of seventeen routines,
Including the Staircase Shuffle and the Delta Stomp.
He has taught three or four white actors in Hollywood.

Snelson lost his left leg in Houston, Texas,
When a truck load of white strikebreakers
Crashed into a Ford containing
Six Negro longshoremen.

Heart's so heavy cain't raise a song,
Heart's so heavy cain't raise a song,
Gonna catch de first train comin' along.

Mr. Heinrich Zangwill discovered Peg Leg Snelson
At a cheap beer garden on Market Street in St. Louis. . . .

Peg Leg Snelson has now
Fifty vivid suits and six high yellow women
And a high-powered roadster.
His wild parties in his Sugar Hill apartment
Cause the preachers to denounce him.
He tips often and he tips big.
He bets on everything . . . everything . . .
From a bedbug race in a honky-tonk
To his ability to make a deacon's wife the first night.

Freemon Hawthorne

When I was a boy in the Ozarks
I used to go into grandfather's barn
To watch old Caesar match his feline cunning
With the cunning of the rats.

One summer there was a drought,
And the rats became desperate with hunger
And withered shadows of themselves.

My grandfather said:
"Keep old Caesar out of the barn . . .
For a hungry rat is a sensible rat."

But when I crawled into my trundle-bed at night
Old Caesar would sneak down to the barn.
One morning I found his remains
In a dark corner,
His bones clean . . . clean as a toothpick.

Coming through the park today,
I saw in the eyes of hungry men
The same look of desperation
That I used to see
In the eyes of the rats
In my grandfather's barn
In the Ozarks.

Joseph Torain

Tracks

My goats leave deep tracks in the mud

They are pregnant

Leslie Ullman

Proof

Soon I will let myself back into the street.
They meet under a speckled canopy
of moonlight.
I am their daughter.

The little girl on their wall grins.
I am the woman in the spare room
peeling off gloves, boots, admiring
my invisible body.

I look like the mistress of the house
when I leave the room. My absence
lacks a shape of its own.

Have I ever lived alone?

I have forgotten
none of my grievances.
The lobster is superb
as is the orchestra, each member
perspires in his tuxedo.
Soon I will let myself back into the street.
A friend will speak of his father's huge hands.
I will enter my parents' house over & over.
I will eat oranges until my skin is flawless.

H. L. Van Brunt

Cerberus

claws on cement
the dog scrapes his chain
up and down the driveway
howling with the sirens
wolf-strong in his throat

asked if love is the answer
he will give that lie his teeth
watch him growl through the freezing rain
and ask yourself if you care
about his cold or chain

Motels, Hotels, Other People's Houses

it seems I was always just a guest
never able to throw
my clothes in a corner
relax on the stool
and read a newspaper
or tell what I really thought
to my hostess about her life
if I sighed too long she thought I was bored
if I didn't want to talk and talk and talk
she wondered why I was there at all
I first felt alien by myself
animals' eyes I couldn't see
in the mountain woods
and sometimes I kicked back at the waves
on the beach at night
as they kicked out at me
I remembered girls
whose hair had streamed
over me like waterfalls
but they might as well have been clouds
I lay always
in the dark alone
where little was said
and less was known

In The Distance

And as I watch the fields
and the mountains
dim in the distance —
the dun-colored fields and the bluish mountains —
and notice, closer,
a spider sleeping
beside a moth —
a small, black spider and a large, white moth —
I see a figure bearing a basket —
as though she were carrying something sacred
to be placed only in my hands,
the shadow of a hood darkens her face,
but I know it is my life she holds —
bits of this and that in a basket.
And as she nears she will turn away.
The only beautiful things on earth
turn into themselves.

Judy Ray

Robert Vander Molen

Sunny

Sunny and not very windy on the shore
I knew her accidently several years before
She wore long hair and there were ladybugs in her hair

And though the season was over (I never knew the date)
There was some activity at the coast guard ramps

There was a dried fish that arched towards the pier

We sat on pieces of driftwood and she smoothed her black hair

And she was edgy because she was late
But it didn't matter
I loved her
The long waves muscled into shore and the trees answered crisply
The water line glistened it was painful

While I kissed her hair I wasn't certain that I was there
Sand blew around our feet and crows blackened the sky
And the road was empty behind us and the town was empty

The coast guard trawlers rocked outward to sea and the station
Itself crumbled and became sand like salt and legends

Byron Vazakas

West Fifty-Seventh Street

(Painting by Robert Henri, 1902)

Inside this street scene frozen in its frame,
an old year's in, my new years yet to come,
as though I'd been here long before my time.

Dark mansions laced with ice wall either side,
but indistinct, as genre art should be,
turned into feeling from a memory.

The stone front steps lead into what has been,
a steeple pointing mist, a horse-drawn cab,
the backs of people who have turned away.

To round the picture off, white smoke clouds bank
above the elevated station where
an era ended in its twilight here.

I came years late, West Fifty-Seventh Street,
into your winterscape that weathers snow
like someone waiting at a rendezvous.

Mark Vinz

Postcards

I. Touring

Yesterday, the
Valley of Fires, today
all pilgrimages end
at the Best Western
in Tucumcari.

There is nothing here

but rocks—beyond
all hope and forgiving.
When no one is watching
we take their pictures.
There's nothing else to do.

Tomorrow we'll probably
decide to wait here awhile.
Maybe someone will come
and take our pictures—
send them on to you.

II. Asylum

It's never lonely here at night.
There's too much to do—
bandaging, stitching, blotting.
Even the lightbulbs bleed.

I'm not allowed to worry you.
They feed us well, keep us
trimmed and exercised.

I'm learning so much
about the fear of falling,
new places to get lost in—
locks, furnaces, the distance,
the gap between your eyes.

III. Homesteader

Somewhere fast trains
howl to each other
through the night valleys.
I dream of them now,
and horses
wild in upland meadows—
moonlight horses
gentle as an old man's tears.

Come visit me—
trains don't stop here anymore,
the mailbox is filling up with snow,
all the fences have been down for years.

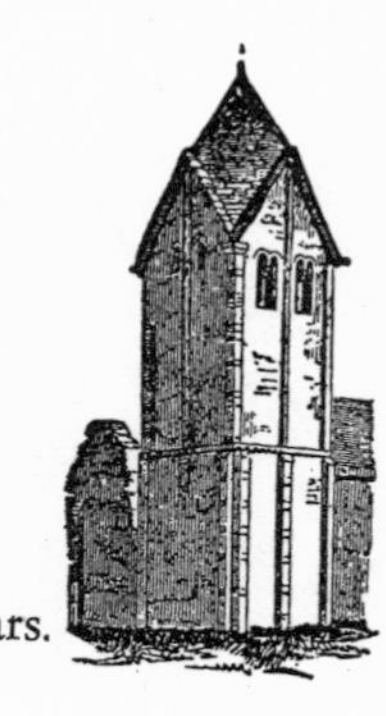

Arturo Vivante

To A Victim Of Radiation

Cecil W. Kelley, died Jan. 1, 1959 at Los Alamos

There were no witnesses when you saw
the blue flash you knew was lethal
and you staggered out of the silent room
to tell your colleagues about it.
They looked at you, whole, with no visible burn,
yet dead in the marrow,
and you looked back at them from the pale of your being.
For a while you seemed well;
your step was light; you could speak without anguish.
But the pale-blue flash went on burning inside you,
stilling the source of your blood
and the well known places,
the laboratories and the familiar faces
began to waver, to dim into oneness,
and you brought your forearm in front of your eyes
to find comfort in darkness.
They fed you with hope of transfusions,
bone marrow grafts, implantations;
volunteers offered you blood,
marrow was flown to you,
but the doctors, your colleagues, you yourself knew
one could only survive a few days
the massive amount of radiation the flash had delivered.
It continued burning inside you,
and strength became weakness,
and heavy the light.
A knot began to close at your throat,
slow, more painful than the knot of the hangman.
Three days you lasted, till the first of the year.
You died the death of an explorer
in the new fields, hostile, invisible, strange.
Your flame was extinguished,
but not the flash.
The pale-blue flash goes on burning inside your bones,
and once you will be ash and we will be ash
it will still go on burning.
Centuries will have to pass
before it will extinguish itself.

Linda Wagner

Love Poem

Isadora, your body charts a course
so filled with light I shade my eyes
as sparks turn flame, you take my
hands, swing me away from sun but
light explodes a set
of radiant planets wheels and
shadows, heaps brilliance under trees
that long for cool/we lie there
there is no way to trace the saffron
light, there is no origin for burns
such as my body bears, there is no sign
no sight, there is no light so calm
as this your silvered body
brings
&
shares

Roger Pfingston

David Wagoner

Relics

. . . the terrible hunger for objects . . .
—Roethke

Leaning against my books, the sunflowers
Wait with their heavy heads bent deeper now
Than when I uprooted them
Cold months ago, their corollas ragged
Around the arcs of seeds, their stalks hardened,
Their leaves as stiff as the broom-stiff roots
Dusting the floor that holds us above ground.

I grew them from the heads of their lost grandfathers
And keep them with me like the gleanings
Of a harvest, for the sake of what *they* keep,
Not weary of time, though ready to do without
The sun, their dazzling, disappearing master,
For as long as I keep this roof over our heads
And keep my own head at the onset of winter.

In my study, while days shorten and darken,
I count what else I've gathered around me:
The goat's jawbone, porcupine teeth, clutches of barnacles,
The nest of a fox sparrow, the slashed wing of a teal,
The stuffed young golden eagle older than I am,
The crosscut slab of cedar from a dead forest,
And these sunflowers, like the relics of ancestors.

Help me now, old goat-beard, slow spiny-back,
Chalk-mouthed sea-eaters, clear singer in thickets,
Marsh-skimmer, sky-toucher, heart of heartwood,
And you sun-gazers, now bent on a long night-watch,
Leaning against my books and pieces of books
And pieces of poems and disembodied words,
Your heads heavy with promises for another season.

Diane Wakoski

For A Man Who Learned To Swim When He Was Sixty

To you,
the ocean was an old mother, saying,
"Leon, why can't you be more like Abe?
He's such a good boy
playing quietly at his little table.

(Leon is such a rascal.
He's never still.)"

And you walk into the blue water,
the sand as white as your mother's ankle.
The palm trees leaning
like old people talking to each other.

Deeper, deeper,
you walk till it's over your waist.

"Leon," calls your mother,
whose voice is now the breakers
crashing out beyond you in the ocean,
beyond this sheltered bay.

"Leon, be careful.
I know you'll do something clever
and get yourself in trouble."

There is no way you can swim.
For sixty years the water speaks
like a mother whom you beautifully obey.
You too, a palm tree, bending to listen carefully
for each word.

Silence
was your answer until one day
there was a different voice.
When you walked into water,

the beautiful white sand was now her braceleted hand,
carressing your feet, making love to your own white body.

I do not really know your story.
But I do know
that at some point the angry voice
her teeth
her stunning white ankle that you feared
became beautiful.

As trophies.
You fought them, possessed them.

It is too simple to say
a woman taught you to swim.

Let us say, instead, that your enemy did.
As the Indians tell us,
it is our enemies/
fighting them/
articulating and defining what we despise or eschew/

our enemies
who make us heroes.

Martha Maverick

David Walker

Catching Up

At thirty-five, I get by
nursing my cramped style: learning

to feel the worm at the root,
the old bone in the foot

charred by much walking; when
things hit me now, part of my flesh

stays bruised, and each morning
more senses crack at the edge.

Much past thirty, it seems
a man grows after his father

too quick— the way a woman
settles to her mother's face

as in a mold: when I last saw
my former wife, I thought

her mother's sister!
Dying's
a little more per more

each week; secretly, we chart it
in our veins, we commission it

by whiskey, lying awake,
lying . . . .
And when I walk

after my father in the field,
the steps I must stumble almost

fail me in his stride.

Mary Wilson

John Wheatcroft

Pisanello's Studies of Men Hanging on Gallows

(Sepia Drawing, the Frick Museum)

Study horror? —without a doubt
from life, the dangling dead, that is,
shamelessly drawing out a shame they've gone beyond,
after pain's last gasp, all of their blood intact.

One fellow's spine hangs exemplary as a plumb line,
a posture for an orthopedic poster.

Another's feet point down and in
quite gracefully, a danseur toeing air.

Behind their backs hands palm to palm,
as praying, resist the last temptation.
Withy bracelets adorning their wrists seem
superfluous. Heads a little forward, as assenting.

The knot in each rope defines the tangle where
reality crosses itself. What matter they're held
forever in suspense? They'll never spoil;
no crow or raven here a breakfast take.

But oh, the heaviness we looking back
at them are made to feel— stalled blood,
breathless flesh, bone on the way to stone.
Now uncorrupted by a choice, a cry, a twitch,
they pledge allegiance to the final force.

One full drawn face must mirror Pisanello
at his work—depersonalized as Caesar,
disinterested as his elsewhere frescoed lady
beneath a green silk canopy
(immaculate her grooming, impeccable
the cabling of her Saxon hair high on
her chin-up head, eyes slyly condescending to
a slew of Arthur's knights below,
battling to the death).

Tucked into two, these four hanged figures
will resurrect themselves in color,
one scarlet doubleted, the other
in scarlet breeches, crumpled down his thighs,
exposing his naked loins to worshipers—
above the Pellegrini Chapel arch
in the church of S. Anastasia, in Verona.

Such ruthless Roman line depicting dead-
weight flesh excites me retrospectively
to pity even that emperor-playing clown
whose skull bulged with north Africa, wired
for finale by the ankles and slung head-down
beside his bloody mistress in a petrol station
across from the muddy town square in Milano.

Sylvia Wheeler

Lost Contact

I am walking the U.S.;
husband follows in the car,
says I'm off my rocker.

I keep to the trees;
he is put off by 'possums
gravel-ground on the road.

He turns for Kingsland;
I bypass to Delight.

After the late, late show,
he phones the Highway Patrol.

They won't leave the highway
for someone off her rocker.

Odds are on rape.

Heather Wilde

Sister Bernardo

O child of sunrise
i see you sit by the window
peeling apples peacefully
all day no complain
no speaka english either
your basket is full
and your knotted fingers run
the course of the core
comically
lightly
your thoughts pour pure as the sea
do not watch television
it would warp you
and you
seeing through half-blind eyes
are so wise
you do not belong to such a world
of violence
and you know
as you pray each night on your
boney knees
that God will take you.
o child of the sunrise
i wish i knew
your secret.

Frederic Will

A fire a simple fire

He is aware of a simple fire.
He follows the dry smoky odor
upward into the forgotten attic.
First he finds nothing.
Then he sees the smoking letter,
a love letter he wrote to his wife.
He tries to extinguish it.
He pours water on it from the sink.
Nothing will put out the growing flames.
Then he runs out in the snow with the letter.
He covers it with shovelsful.
But the snow begins smoking.
He carries a shovel of snow with the letter,
takes them to the well,
heaves them to the bottom.
Then he closes the well.
Forever after the water tastes fiery.

Judy Ray

Jonathan Williams

In Lucas, Kansas

(for Clarence John Laughlin)

Samuel Perry Dinsmoor
built a "Garden of Eden"
containing
among other things
trees, sidewalks, fences, flower beds,
fish pool,
bird and animal cages,
U.S. flags,
a "Goddess of Liberty,"
soldier, Indian, animals, birds,
a monument showing
"The Crucifixion of Labor,"
angels, the Devil,
Adam & Eve,
the Serpent,
Cain & Abel,
and a visitors'
dining hall.

All these things
are constructed in cement
and by 1927
he had used over 113 tons
or about
2273 sacks
of cement.

Photo by
Glenn R.
Fulton

PLACE STAMP
HERE

Robert Willson

The Last Resort

We came for luck,
Restoring passion
On twenty a day for
Underdone eggs and nude swims.
Hunched in a boat,
Lakeside Bill and Coo,
We fished at dawn
For more than bass:
Hooks were baited with
Souvenirs, mementos,
Words of apology.
No one felt a tug.

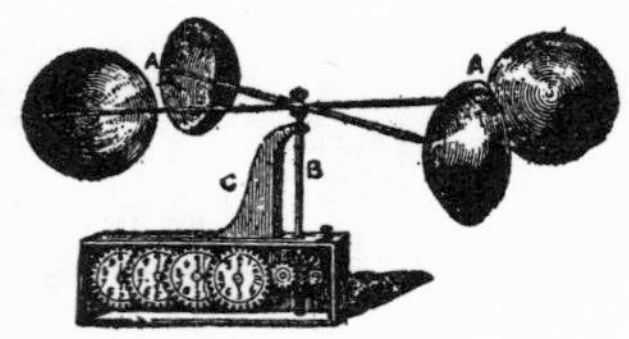

Harold Witt

Superbull

The bull's excited by another bull
and then they lead him to a fraudulent cow—
nothing but cowhide over an empty shell
with a man inside carefully holding out
a plastic vagina. Pasiphae's Taurus,
the ballheavy animal magnificently mounts,
his hind hooves clanging like the Anvil Chorus
as his long pink penis pulses and pounds.
What a trick to play on that dumb beast
by selective breeders collecting superior semen—
I, for one, would rather eat less meat
or dine on organic vegetables than see him
fucking a fiction that never had a teat,
and robbed of his real function, like some men.

Valerie Worth

Body

all the
outward and the inward

the pearl of oil
in the ear-
lamp
the slip of
black lakes
behind sight

the writhing
wands and the slicks
breathing

the cluster-combs
the caverns
and spouts

everywhere
salt and ivory
prickle and slab

even in
sleep
the swashes
and feasts

all the hermetic
and all the
unsealed

all the
richly kept
and the richly given
away

Charles David Wright

Some Semblance of Order

Ask what delights you in dancing,
and number will reply, 'Lo, here am I.'
St. Augustine, *de libero arbitrio,* II. xvi. 42.

Others made danceroom for us, she was so fine.
The lead guitarist by his shrug of eyebrows
and the straight word of his hips conceded
more than was true. There in the Starlite Lounge,
only in the dance had I cut him out,
only in the dance I had picked her up
(whatever passionate scenario moved me)
and I, more truly, was the one picked up—
up from the bar stool, up from the passionate
scenario I projected, up into her dancing.
We danced on that small circle, I only the Earth
(of our lost worldpicture); around me she sphered
in lovely epicycles, turning as she turned,
my earthy bugaloo only her plain ground, around
me moved the water, air, fire and circled order
of her abandon. It was not an act, it was *the* act,
the Natural Act. The floor became the bed
that she was good in. That so much exquisite
indirection in all directions could say simply
one thing: her body making and being made,
her body drawing mine into making it,
that this many wheeling moves (each breast
in its own orbit, her hips on either side
sidereal, her hands wandering like planets
over the planes of our imagined bodies being made,
her head ever inclining new angles of incident light)
could fly to waste upon that waxed Congoleum
spun me between lust and wonder.

Suddenly, finding some other compass than my cock,
I followed her as she unmade that bed
to which I had read all her motions motioning.
Up from her knees in ones and twos and threes
I, she and I, we and the lead guitarist
rose beyond who with whom, the order of her act
shining
beyond the act, a symmetry of any number
dancing.

Paul Zimmer

Lester Tells of Wanda and the Big Snow

Some years back I worked a strip mine
Out near Tylersburg. One day it starts
To snow and by two we got three feet.
I says to the foreman, "I'm going home."
He says, "Ain't you staying till five?"
I says, "I have to see to my cows,"
Not telling how Wanda was there at the house.
By the time I make it home at four
Another foot is down and it don't quit
Until it lays another. Wanda and me
For three whole days seen no one else.
We tunneled the drifts, we slid
Right over the barbed wire and laughed
At how our heartbeats melted the snow.
After a time the food was gone and I thought
I would butcher a cow, but then it cleared
And the moon come up as sweet as an apple.
Next morning the ploughs got through. It made us sad.
It don't snow like that no more. Too bad.

HAIKU

by Richard Wright

The crow flew so fast
That he left his lonely caw
Behind in the fields

Just enough of rain
To bring the smell of silk
From the umbrellas

Coming from the woods
A bull has a sprig of lilac
Dangling from a horn

Why is the hail so wild
Bouncing so frighteningly
Only to lie so still

A balmy spring wind
Reminding me of something
I cannot recall

Haiku by Richard Wright

The dog's violent sneeze
Fails to rouse a single fly
On his mangy back

I would like a bell
Tolling this soft twilight
Over willow trees

The green cockleburs
Caught in the thick wooly hair
Of the black boy's head

Winter rain at night
Sweetening the taste of bread
And spicing the soup

An empty sickbed
An indented white pillow
In weak winter sun